110 REDEMPTION ROAD

From 6+ Life Sentences to Freedom

David Spicer

WWW.TRUEVINEPUBLISHING.ORG

110 Redemption Road
David Spicer

Published by
True Vine Publishing Company
810 Dominican Dr.
Nashville TN 37228
www.TrueVinePublishing.org

ISBN: 978-1-968092-33-7 Paperback
ISBN: 978-1-968092-34-4 eBook

Printed in the United States of America.
For information, contact the author.

TABLE OF CONTENTS

INTRODUCTION

Lessons Learned the Hard Way

From a man who is 46 years old at time of writing this, I have spent twenty seven of those years in some of America's toughest prisons, both state and federal, including over nine years in the infamous federal juggernaut ADX Florence, Colorado, nicknamed *The Alcatraz of the Rockies*, where inmates commit suicide more than any other federal prison.

I have met some of Al-Qaeda's terrorists who wanted to kill Americans like the "shoebomber" Richard Reid also, coming face to face with American terrorist Terry Nichols, who helped Oklahoma City bomber Timothy McVeigh build the bomb that was used to murder 168 trusting men, women and children—injuring another 500 more. I lived in a cell next to founder of the Gangster Disciples, Larry Hoover and met the leader of the Black Peace Stones, Jeff Fort, who was charged with trying to murder Americans, by blowing up an airline for Libyan President Gaddafi.

I hope you will enjoy reading this redemption story from a formal gang leader, who was sentenced to six life sentences plus thirty years and is now a free man.

CHAPTER 1

EARLY YEARS

My first real memories go back to 1975. I was five years old, living in Mississippi. That year left a mark on me I still feel.

Christmas Eve was always big in our house. The smell of my mother's cooking filled every corner, cakes and pies from scratch, pots bubbling, the oven working overtime. She was a real cook, no shortcuts. On that night she always gave me something special. When she finished whipping the cake batter, she handed me the beater. I would lick it clean, the sweet taste sitting heavy on my tongue. She did the same for my brothers and sisters, but when she called my name it felt different. She asked, "How does it taste?" I answered, "Good." Simple words, but they made me feel like I mattered.

Later that night she called me back into the kitchen. The lights seemed dimmer, the air heavier. My three older brothers leaned against the counter, grinning. Something in their smiles told me this was serious. My mother sat at the table, face lit with a wide grin, eyes sparkling. She took my hands and said she had a secret.

"You cannot tell your little sister," she said.

"Yes, ma'am," I answered.

"There is no Santa Claus."

The words stung. I pulled my hands back. She explained that my father was the one who ate the cake and pie, and that she and my dad put the toys under the tree after we went to bed.

That night they let me stay up. I watched my father walk back and forth from their bedroom with boxes of toys, placing each one under the tree. My mother kept glancing at me, smiling like she wanted to make sure I was all right. My father sat down and ate the cookies and pie. Nobody spoke. The clock ticked. It was the latest I had ever stayed awake.

My mind spun. I thought about every Christmas before when I jumped out of bed, ran through the house, and yelled, "Santa Claus came!" Those memories felt different now. At five I did not know the word trust, but I knew something had cracked. Even the weatherman on TV who tracked Santa across the map felt like a lie. It seemed like everybody had been in on it.

From that night on, Christmas never felt the same. Year after year we pass this story to our kids as truth, then expect them to always tell the truth. Why not just tell them what it is really about? Christmas is about the birth of Jesus Christ.

Every Christmas Eve around six, the weatherman would point to a radar map and say where Santa was. I was more upset with him than with my parents, because he did not just talk, he showed it. Rudolph, the red-nosed reindeer we all knew by name, went through trials too. He got treated wrong for being different. The whole season was full of stories, and I started to wonder which ones were real.

For years Christmas turned into stuff, sales, new Jordans, spending more and calling it a holiday. We say we celebrate Jesus while we treat it like a party. The Bible says in Jeremiah 10:1–5:

"Hear ye the word which the Lord speaketh unto you, O house of Israel. Thus saith the Lord, Learn not the way of the heathen, and be not dismayed at the signs of heaven; for the heathen are dismayed at them. For the customs of the people are vain: for one cutteth a tree out of the forest, the work of the hands of the workman, with the axe. They deck it with silver and with gold; they fasten it with nails and with hammers, that it move not. They are upright as the palm tree, but speak not: they must needs be borne, because they cannot go. Be not afraid of them, for they cannot do evil, neither also is it in them to do good."

You can tell yourself there is no harm in it, but what will you say to God on Judgment Day? We did not stop at Christmas. We turned holy days into holidays because they made us feel good. What does Easter, the celebration of Jesus rising from the dead on Resurrection Sunday, have to do with a bunny and eggs? Then we wonder why America is in the shape it is in.

By early 1976 I was still five, counting down to six because six meant school. I was in the hallway when I heard my mom and dad arguing in the kitchen. I had never heard them speak to each other like this. The kitchen light spread across the linoleum. I peeked around the corner. Boiling water bubbled in a pot on the stove as words flew between them, sharp and fast.

I'm not sure what my mom said, but in the blink of an eye, my father charged at my mom, picking up the scolding hot water and dowsing my mother with it. My mother screamed and fell to the ground while my father continued to hit her with the red hot pan.

Her dress melted into her skin where the water hit. I could not move. My brothers rushed in, grabbing my father's arms, pulling, shouting. The smell of scorched cloth and hot metal filled my nose. I watched, rooted to the spot, while the life I thought I knew shook itself apart on our floor.

A white police officer came to the house and talked to my parents. Surprisingly, my dad did not go to jail. My mother could not press charges, even with the horrific wounds on her body.

Now that I am older, I understand more about that time and place. In the deep south, Black men often did not go to jail for beating their wives. Black women often did not go to the hospital to have babies. There was no money. There was no help. There was only survival.

The officer left that night and the next day came like it always does. My mother never took a day off from being a mother. She was hurt, but she kept the house running. She fed us. She was the queen.

After that day I never once heard her talk about what happened with my father. Not long after, life kept coming. The midwife was cheap, an older woman from the neighborhood who had helped deliver babies before. Folks called it experience, but it was women doing the best they could with what they had. One Sunday, September 20, 1976, my mother felt like she had to use the bathroom. She sat down, called out, then rolled off the toilet onto the floor. The baby came right there on the bathroom tiles. That is how the story was told in our house. We cleaned up and kept it moving. That was life where we lived.

My mother used to say that out of her eleven children, I was the easiest at first and later the one who gave her the most headaches.

My father left in 1985, but my mother loved him until she died on September 21, 2012. She never remarried. She raised ten other children without help from any man or woman. Her belt was legendary. She did not swing to injure, just enough to make her children straighten up and fly right, like she said.

I salute you, Mrs. Minnie Lee Spicer. For years, the strongest Black woman most people will never know. I am proud and honored to be your child. You made me proud.

You are not forgotten. I love you deeply and dearly. Thank you for forty-two years of unconditional love.

I wrote the following poem on February 21, 2013:

"It Was Mama"
It was Mama who taught me to kneel,
And pray in times of deep trouble,
That is what gives me peace to this day.

When I was ill, it was Mama who
 Cooked hot meals
 That made me heal.

It was Mama who, with a simple hug,
Gave and taught me how to love.

Even though Mama has gone on to her
Heavenly home in the sky, I can
Still smell her pecan pie. I know
She is baking for the angels and for God
Above. Thank you, Mama, for forty-two years of
Unconditional love.

It was Mama who I can still hear say,
 "Did you forget to pray?"

CHAPTER 2

MOM AND DAD SEPARATE

When mama and dad separated, I did not understand much. I only knew mama moved us in with her mother, a woman she barely spoke to. We called her "Mader." I cannot tell you how long we stayed there. It was not long. I slept on the hallway floor with a thin blanket and my shoes as a pillow.

"Wake up," Joe whispered one morning. "I just saw my dad's truck. I am going home."

Even now, older, I can hear the way he said it, like home was something you could claim by willpower alone.

Mama loved us with a heavy kind of love. She tried to keep a family together that had already cracked. She loved my father deeply and loved us deeper. My father was a disabled Navy vet who received a government check every month. I imagine Mama at her mother's table, counting mouths and dollars, knowing she could not stay. Mader was tough. There was not much room for pride or sympathy.

We moved back home. By then we were not afraid of my father the way we had been. I think he knew it, and I think he told himself none of it was his fault.

My father was a strange kind of normal. He always carried a pistol in his front pocket, the grip sticking out plain as day. No holster. No attempt to hide it. When he sat, the gun rested within easy reach. He wore slacks or khakis, a dress shirt, cowboy boots, and a hat. I cannot remember him in blue jeans or a T-shirt. He watched TV preachers, Muhammad Ali fights, and old cowboy movies on a little black-and-white set with a wire hanger for an antenna. We were not allowed to make noise when those shows came on. We better not so much as sneeze.

On Saturday mornings I used pliers to turn the TV knob and watched Jungle Quest, Yogi Bear, and whatever cartoons I could catch. I ate sweet cornflakes on the floor and felt, for a minute, like a regular kid.

My father always had a hustle. Roadside vegetables, odd jobs, little schemes with neighbors. Nothing held. That stop-and-start life taught me to watch faces and read the room. I learned to spot the smile that covered anger and to step back before it broke.

Outside was where I could breathe. I ran, climbed trees, chased U-Hauls down the block, and imagined us moving somewhere better. I wanted money, not to stunt, but to choose. The older I got, the quicker my temper came. Childhood felt like it was sliding past, and I could not catch hold.

When Mama decided to leave, she moved in silence. Daddy took his truck in early. She sent us to school like it was any other morning, then gave us our signal.

"If you see my car outside," she said at the door, "stand up, tell the teacher you need to go, and walk out."

That is exactly what we did. One moment we sat in class. The next we were in the hallway, then the parking lot, then on the highway, making our escape.

We drove to Pine Bluff, Arkansas, where our older brother worked. He had no idea we were coming. We found him at Fred's Dollar Store, where he was manager. When my brother and I walked in, his face went from confusion to shock to a kind of soft relief.

"What are y'all doing here," he said, voice low.

"Mama is outside," I said.

He came to the car. A few minutes later he said, "Stay the night. We will figure it out in the morning."

The next morning the plan settled into place. I would stay with my older brother. One of my brothers would stay as well. Mama, my sisters, and the little boys would go to a shelter for abused women. We were told we could not stay there. We were too old.

When Mama and my sister took the two little ones to the shelter, a sadness hit me I could not explain. The only other times I had been away from her were when she went to the hospital to have a baby. I do not remember the shelter's name, only the big two-way mirror in the entry. I want to say thank you to that place, even now.

Mama stayed there a week and found a small house to rent. We all moved in. I enrolled in school and went out for football. The coaches liked my "Yes, ma'am" and "Yes, sir," the way I was raised to speak. Being the new kid made me interesting. People wanted to know who I was. For a moment, that felt good.

That night, in the bare living room of the rental, we sat on the floor. A single lamp lit the corner. Boxes were stacked like small walls. Mama had that tired look that is more than tired. She rested her hands on her knees and spoke soft.

"I need y'all to understand why we left."

We were quiet.

She said, "I found your daddy's .22. You know the little rifle he keeps tucked away."

Joe frowned. "The one he wrapped for Christmas one year."

"The same one," she said. "I check it sometimes. It is always empty. This time it was not."

"What you mean not," my brother said.

"Not empty," she said. "Loaded. A full set of bullets in it. I looked at that gun, and I heard God. I heard, 'Minnie, get up. Take your children. Go.'"

I felt my chest pull tight. "Mama, you think he would have used it."

She looked at each of us in turn. "I think I was not going to wait to find out. I will not lose a child because I stayed when God said move."

My sister whispered, "So that is why you told us to walk out of school."

"Yes," Mama said. "I needed time and I needed quiet. Your daddy has wrapped that same rifle as a gift before. He thinks that kind of thing is funny. I do not."

She let the words sit. Then she said, "I love your father. I always will. But I love you deeper. We are going to build something new. It will not be easy. It will be ours."

No one spoke after that. The little house creaked and settled. Outside, a car passed and the light slid across the wall.

People tell stories about gangs that make for easy TV. They say kids join because love is missing at home, or because both parents are strung out, or because poverty crushes everything. Sometimes that is true. Often it is not. We were not in a war zone like El Salvador where joining a gang might mean the difference between eating and starving. In Pine Bluff I saw boys not much older than me with cars, cash, and clean outfits. I wanted that. They wanted me for my size.

Back in Mississippi I had gone to a school where first grade through twelfth grade shared one building. White kids went to their school. Black kids went to ours. I had never attended school with white kids. I had never even heard the word marijuana. In Arkansas I sat in class with white kids, played football with them, and stood on the same sidewalks passing the same joint. It did not take long before someone asked me to join up.

We stood behind the gym when they put it to me plain.

"You trying to run with us," one boy said.

"What I got to do," I asked.

"Walk the line," he said. "Start at that end. Do not fall."

They formed two rows facing each other. I stepped into the space between them. I walked forward while fists and open hands slammed into my shoulders and ribs. By the end my eye was swelling and my lip was cut. I spit blood and laughed like it was brave.

"How I am going to tell Mama," I said to myself on the walk home.

That night she looked at me hard. "What happened to your face."

"Football," I said.

She held my eyes for a long time, then nodded once. I felt the lie sit heavy in my mouth. If gangs were really about love and family, we would not need to hide them from the people who actually love us.

I did not need a gang to feel like I belonged. The boys had already made me feel cool before the initiation. Plenty of kids hung around without joining. But once I was in, the fights started. Colors. Corners. Oaths. Blocks none of us owned. Streets we did not pay taxes on. I knew boys who got killed for wearing the wrong color or being on the wrong side of town. How fucked up that is. We call ourselves civilized. We call this the land of the free.

If I could go back and change it, I would. I cannot. What I can do is tell it straight. Situations change. Feelings change. Sometimes in days, sometimes in years. Yesterday is history, and that is why they call it the past. Today is a gift, the present. Tomorrow is a mystery promised to no one. So let us stop the stuck-on-stupid routine and live with our eyes open.

Mama taught us to respect elders, to never hurt women or children, and to treat people the way we wanted to be treated.

"Do you hear me," she would say, palms open, eyes steady.

"Yes, ma'am," we would answer.

I heard her then. I hear her now. Even when I was off track, her words kept knocking on the door.

CHAPTER 3

BACK TO REALITY

We had settled into life, and to me it felt good. Arkansas fit. I did not think about my dad much. If I did, it was a quick thought that passed like a car on the highway.

We had been there six or seven months when my father found us. He called. He showed up. He worked on Mama's heart the way only he knew how. "Come home," he said. "We can fix it." I do not know everything he told her, but I know what happened next. We packed again.

Leaving Arkansas felt like waking up in the middle of a dream. One day we were making new friends and running new streets. The next day we were loading the car. "Tell your brother goodbye," Mama said. I hugged him tight outside Fred's Dollar Store and felt the old life climb back into the car with us.

I brought my new self home. I dressed different. I thought I was cool. I talked with new slang, leaned when I walked, carried a little limp that I thought looked tough. I was hip-hop. You could not tell me anything.

Parents need to understand something. When you uproot your kids and move around, then bring them back, you might slide back into your old life without much friction. Nine out of ten times your child will not. Our brains are still changing. If you pull us out of a bad place into a better one, then drop us back into the same old mess, that is a kind of trauma. Folks shrug and say, "Whatever, at least I did not kill you." That is not the bar.

I was happy in Arkansas. I felt like somebody. My voice had more weight. My height did too. People noticed when we returned to Mississippi. It felt like leaving the city for the country, then being told to act like the country never left you.

"Boy," an uncle said when he saw me, "you cityfied now."

"I am proper now," I joked, half serious.

"Where that yes, sir went," he asked, laughing.

"It is still here," I said, but I said it with a smile I used when I did not plan to change.

In Mississippi I was still a boy under my parents' eyes. Outside of that, the ground had shifted. Overnight a handful of us were calling ourselves a crew. We were not a real gang the way I had seen in Pine Bluff, but we acted like we knew something. We wore our hats a certain way. We had signs and handshakes, secrets that made us feel bigger than the town.

Arkansas had shown me another way people lived. I always thought everyone had rats and roaches like we did. Seeing clean kitchens and a different kind of quiet changed me. It helped and it hurt. The good part was I could name what I wanted. The bad part was I never wanted to be poor again.

We did not get allowances. In a poor household you worked. I washed whites for ten dollars when I could. I handed Mama five and kept five. It taught me to count and it taught me to want. Wanting turned into edge. I started getting in trouble. Fights at school. One day I stabbed a boy in the arm. I am not proud of it. I was angry most days, and walking that anger around like it was mine to carry.

My father was a disabled veteran. He did not have to work and rarely left the house. By then he and I were into it all the time. I did not speak to him unless I had to. He did not like the man I was trying to be. I did not like the man he was. I had grown to six foot three. He stood six feet even. The fact that he had to tip his chin up to look at me and I had to drop mine to look at him did not help.

"Watch your tone," he would say.

"Then watch yours," I would answer.

Mama would step between us. "Both of you, enough," she said, palms out. "This is my house."

One afternoon on the field a boy said, "We need money."

"For what," I asked.

"For everything," he said. "Shoes. Gas. Life."

A plan took shape the way those plans do, fast and wrong. We knew we could not hit anyone in our own town. Too many uncles and cousins, too many folks who knew whose child you were. On weekends I caddying for golf players, men with money. Everyone knew golf players were rich by our measure. That was the crowd we watched.

"Not here," I said. "Somewhere else."

"Somewhere they will not know our names," another boy said.

We nodded like we were running a business instead of running toward a bad choice. I did not know it then, but lines were being drawn. Childhood on one side, whatever came next on the other.

At night I lay in bed and stared at the ceiling. Arkansas felt like a movie I had walked out of too early. Mississippi felt like a movie I had seen too many times. I kept hearing Mama in my head. "Respect elders. Do not hurt women or children. Treat people the way you want to be treated." I wanted to be that boy. I also wanted the money and the weight that came with it. Those two wants do not mix.

"Son," Mama said one evening, catching me by the door, "sit down a minute."

"Yes, ma'am."

She studied my face. "You look like you are carrying something."

"I am fine."

"You do not have to tell me everything," she said. "But tell God the truth. That is where help starts."

I nodded. I wanted to say more. I did not. I stood up and kissed her forehead. "I hear you."

She squeezed my hand. "Make sure you do."

Back in my room I counted the cash I had from cutting grass and small jobs. It was not much. It felt like everything and nothing at the same time. The plan was still out there, waiting.

"Tomorrow," a boy said the next day, low and quick. "We move tomorrow."

I looked at him, then past him, to the road that ran out of town. I had learned in Arkansas that life could be different. Now I had to learn whether I would let that truth change me, or whether I would change the truth to fit what I wanted.

The sun went down. The night came on. Mississippi air is heavy after dark. It sat on my skin like a decision I had not made yet.

CHAPTER 4

FIRST TIME IN JAIL

I was the one who always felt I had to prove I was not afraid. Inside, I was.

I slipped onto the golf course at St. Paul through the back entrance and spotted a lone golfer playing by himself. When he teed off, I saw his wallet and watch sitting in the cart.

"Now," I told myself.

I ran for it, snatching his wallet, but not before he saw me and gave chase. We fought. I wanted his wallet. He was not letting it go. He smashed my hand with a golf club, splitting the skin on the back. Blood poured and my hand swelled fast.

I took off and beat him back to the car. In the seat I wrapped my hand in a car coat and tried to breathe through the pain. Inspite of my near capture, I had hit a jackpot: Five hundred dollars. We hit a store for a bag of ice. I flexed my fingers. Not broken. Maybe a bad fracture. I could feel enough to keep moving. I gave the two guys in the car one hundred each. Three hundred left. It was the most money I had ever held. I told myself I was rich. That is how naïve I was. I had no idea that five hundred would cost me far more over the years.

We went to the mall where I bought clothes and shoes like the money would never end. I did not think for one second about explaining any of it to my parents. I did not get the chance. Before I got home, the police had come by and told them they were looking for me. Word spread through the neighborhood. I did not go home. I was not going to jail.

I had a little more than one hundred left. I bought a one-way bus ticket to Arkansas for fifty-three dollars. Once I got there I learned fast that life on the run is no piece of cake. My father called my older brother, told him what I had done, and told him not to let me stay. I was sixteen with no I.D. I could not rent a room. I did not know how to hustle a clerk. Most of my clothes were back home in plastic bags.

On my second day I fell asleep outside my brother's apartment building. A security guard woke me up and told me I had to leave. I felt so alone. Later, a friend let me crawl through a window and crash on the floor for a couple of hours. Being in a hard spot will humble you. With nowhere to go, I did the one thing that made sense to me. I went to school. Back to the same school I had attended when we lived in Arkansas.

I sat by the main office, drifted through the halls, and visited old teachers who had no clue what I had done. They were happy to see me anyway. To all of you, especially you, Mrs. Riley, I never forgot your kindness.

From the school phone I called Mama. She was crying and begging me to come home. She said she had talked to the police and they promised if I turned myself in I would get probation, no jail time. I said I would try.

A kid at school told me a way to get back to Mississippi without money. He laid out how it worked.

"The Greyhound bus drivers pick up mail and drop it off in other states," he explained. "All you have to do is wait for the bus to come pick up the mail. When the driver goes in to get the mail, you sneak into the bus and go to the bathroom. Don't lock it though, because it will show that the bathroom is occupied. Just shut the door and sit on the toilet, just in case someone walks in."

So that's what I did. I pulled my pants down and sat on the toilet, looking like I was using the restroom. Low and behold it worked. I rode that Greyhound bus all the way from Pine Bluff, Arkansas to Jackson, MS. Thank you Mr. Bus Driver for not checking that bathroom.

Back in Mississippi I tried to call Mama, but I couldn't reach her. I asked around the station and got nothing until I ran into someone from my neighborhood. They said there had been train wreck which led to a chemical spill. The people in the community had to evacuate. It was on the four o'clock news. I had missed it. Mama had gone to St. Louis.

I walked to my grandfather's house, but he met me at the door. "Your brother called," he said. "Told me what you did. You cannot stay here."

Anger hit me like heat. I turned around and walked back to the bus station. I pretended to wait for a bus so I could sleep in a chair. For three days I went without food. I walked the streets in daylight and came back to that same chair at night. Looking back, if I had any sense I would have turned myself in right then.

I finally went to my friend's house—who helped me with the robbery, where my father came to pick me up. In the car I told him the truth. He did not say much, but I could tell he was angry. He drove me to the jail on a Friday. I walked in and turned myself in. It is not easy when you are sixteen and unaware as hell.

Booking was the kind of humiliation that sticks. "Pull your cheeks apart." "Lift your balls." I stood barefoot on a cold cement floor with shame in my throat. They moved me to the juvenile side. The first questions out of the guard's mouth was, "what drugs are you on?"

That day, they gave us leftover dinner and a bologna sandwich. To this day I hate bologna.

I had court the next morning. Since I was a juvenile, I could have gone home if a parent agreed to be responsible. My father stood, looked at the judge, and said he would not be responsible for me. I was sent back to jail. I was locked up for twenty-one days. My dad had left town, my momam was in St. Louis. I was cut off. No cake. No visit. Just time and my thoughts.

After he left, Mama spoke to the judge and said she would be responsible. That was it. I was free. It was a Friday. I remember because on the ride home Mama said my football coaches wanted me suited up for the game that night.

I took a shower and went to school with only a few hours of jail washed off me. When a kid gets out of jail, everybody knows. People treated me like a rock star. I guess because even as children we hear the horror stories and believe anyone who makes it through must be tough. If they only knew how scared I was.

CHAPTER 5

BURYING THE DEVIL

The next week, on Thursday, we had film day. We watched the team we would face on Friday. We met in the library because it had air-conditioning and the locker room did not. I saw my mother's car pull up with two of my brothers, so I stood, walked out to the front steps, and met them there. My mother's voice was steady when she said, "Your daddy died."

Inside, I felt a rush of relief and a strange quiet at the same time, but I kept my face flat for her sake because I knew how deeply she loved him. The last time he and I spoke, I told him, "Next time you show up here, you are in it," and I meant every word. In that moment I could have jumped for joy, because it felt like my prayer had been answered, but I did not show it.

I never cried for my father, not on that day and not since. Parents who never tell some of their children "I love you" should not be surprised when those children do not mourn. Looking back, I know I was hurt. I loved my mother, and I wanted to be loved by him as well. I waited for the four words a son needs—"I love you, son"—and they never came.

He never played catch with us or came to a single game. Anything that was not manual labor was dismissed as nonsense. Birthdays meant one dollar, no matter how old we were. When school let out for summer, I got up early just to be gone before he woke. I picked blackberries while the dew was still on them, chopped cotton until my back ached, split firewood and sold it by the cord, cut grass, and roamed the woods. I brought a few dollars home to my mother and kept a little for myself, then ate, showered, and slept. That is how I learned to survive under his roof.

When a father tells a boy, "I should have flushed you down the toilet," and "You are not going to be anything," hate becomes the only clean emotion that seems to make sense. Some of my family blamed his wife for how he acted, but I was fifteen and stubborn, and I trusted what I saw with my own eyes.

I was required to attend the funeral, which felt like a bad joke. Aside from family, perhaps five people showed up. This is the kind of moment that can turn young people off church altogether. A preacher who never met my father stood over the casket and talked about Heaven like he knew the guest list. He said, "He is in a better place," and then laid out a neat path of good neighbors, good deeds, and a guaranteed spot beyond the clouds. By that standard, I wondered where my father was headed. The man did not know him; he simply knew the script.

The service felt like a performance because that is what funerals too easily become. In the fellowship hall there was potato salad, cakes, and pies. People who never knew the dead lined up for free plates. Gossip rose around the punch bowl. The preacher recited, "Ashes to ashes and dust to dust," and the room hummed "Amen," before the crowd drifted to the food. Too often a funeral is judged like a party: plenty of food, plenty of talk, and not much truth.

They called his name. They closed the box. We walked outside into the heat. I stood beside my mother because that is what a son does. I did it for her, not for him. In the car she stared out the window, and I watched her profile and thought about the weight she carried that none of us could see. She loved him to the end and still kept us alive, and that was the math that mattered.

At the house someone said, "He is gone on to glory." I said nothing. In my head I answered that God could sort that out. I had my own reckoning to do. Putting him in the ground was not going to bury what he planted in me. That would take years, and it might take a lifetime.

That night I lay in bed and listened to the quiet while the field lights from the school flickered across the ceiling. I could still hear the coach's voice breaking down plays, and I could still hear my mother on the steps saying, "Your daddy died." The words sat between us like a closed door. I knew that someday I would have to open it and walk through, whether I wanted to or not.

In the morning I laced my cleats and went to practice. Life kept moving: school, drills, the same streets, and the same choices. People patted my shoulder and told me to stay strong, and I nodded because strength felt like a mask that kept me from explaining what lived underneath it.

The devil they buried that week had my last name, and what he left behind had mine too. I would have to decide which man I intended to be.

I really don't have but one memory of my life after my dad's funeral. I lost my virginity. It was nothing special and then trouble came knocking again. I was emotionally dead. I was moving, talking, and planning, but my heart was numb. I did not cry. I did not ask for help. I just kept going, acting like nothing touched me–It did. It touched everything, and the cost of pretending I was fine turned out to be a bill I did not know I was making my mother pay.

My mother, God bless her, taught us right from wrong. She said to tell the truth, keep our hands to ourselves, and respect elders. What could not teach me was the full weight of consequences.

People warn you that trouble can lead to jail or even death, but no one looks you in the eye and says, "If you do this, it will break your mother's back. It will chew through her savings, send her begging for a lawyer she can not afford, and take food out of your brothers' mouths. It will put put

110 R<small>EDEMPTION</small> R<small>OAD</small>

her on a highway for eight hundred miles round trip to sit in courtrooms holding her breath every time the judge calls your name."

That was the part I did not understand. I thought I was slick. I told myself, "I will not get caught. I am faster than luck and smarter than rules." Then I got caught, and the nights felt like a movie scene that would not end, the same nightmare on a loop. Sleep would start, then stop, then start again, and every time I woke, the problem was still there, sitting on my chest.

I lived through it, but I missed what it was doing to my life. Juvenile court handed me two years of probation. I had already spent twenty-one days locked up, and I kept thinking about the five hundred dollars that started it all. That little hit turned into court costs and fees that ran my mother two thousand dollars. She was a single parent by then. I told myself I would stay out of trouble for the full two years, partly because I was scared straight, partly because I was walking around in a daze.

I was not born a bad kid. I was a bored kid with no father and too much empty space. In a small town there is only so much to do. When school ends, the world gets quiet and the streets get loud. Life did not feel like it had meaning. I did not have a mentor. I did not even know what a role model was. Time slipped by. I remember very little after my father's funeral. I lost my virginity. It was nothing special, just another thing I did because it was there to do. Then trouble found me again and knocked like it owned the door.

What I know now is simple. Consequences are not just jail time and fines. Consequences are your mother praying herself hoarse because she cannot sleep. They are your brothers eating less because the light bill is due. They are the way your name sounds when it is said by a judge, by a coach, by a teacher who used to be proud of you. They are the weight that turns a boy's face older than his years.

CHAPTER 6

SEVENTEEN AND OUT OF CONTROL

At seventeen I had access to two cars: my mother's sedan and my older brother's dusty Buick that sat near the edge of the store lot. Parents trust their kids more than they should sometimes. Mine did enough to hand over keys. Two sets of wheels felt like two hall passes. Freedom multiplied.

Freedom also multiplies the chances to mess up. I rode city buses and cut through new corners, met people who lived the life I thought I wanted. After a couple of years feeling emotionally dead and numb in my body, I slid into a crowd that moved the way I was moving. We were not hunting people to hurt. Most of us still showed respect to elders, said "Yes, sir" and "Yes, ma'am," and held doors like we had been taught. I was introverted by nature. With the right guidance I might have stayed quiet and clean. Without it, I did what too many teenagers do with too much time and too little purpose. I got into trouble.

It started small. It usually does. A grab here, a lift there. Shoplifting turned into a habit. Time sped up the more we did it. Each time I got away with something, the next time felt easier. I grew bold. I started testing boundaries that did not need testing. I convinced myself it was nothing because the items were small. That is how people lie to themselves. Wrong is wrong.

I kept lines in my head about how far I would go, and I told myself I would not cross them. Being a juvenile made me reckless. In our town most first-time offenders caught a lecture and a paper cut of a punishment. I learned the wrong lesson from that. I thought the system could not really touch me. That idea fed my arrogance.

The truth is stealing does something to your mind. It turns patience into a blade and attention into a net. For a few minutes you feel sharp and alive. Then it fades, and you are emptier than before, chasing the next little jolt. I was doing dumb things for quick feelings that never lasted.

The more I pressed my luck, the more luck ran out. Trouble came back wearing steel. A weapon entered the picture, and the game I thought I was playing turned into something else entirely.

***

"Two-eleven in progress."

That was the soundtrack in Jackson in 1986 and 1987. Guns were easy. Everybody knew somebody who had more than one. Drug murders spiked. Big-name gang members got shot by rivals, and carloads of six young men rolled the streets looking for each other. Cops were pulling folks over faster than they could write the reports. Most nights ended downtown for questioning. That was the rhythm.

We were not part of those murders, but we told ourselves we needed heat to protect ourselves. A friend's mother bought a handgun at a pawn shop. Once we were strapped, we rode more. You circle a city long enough with nothing to do and the streets start talking to you. Unemployed time turns into a loaded chamber. Add fear and ego. Click. Then the only thing left to do is shoot shit into the air because you can, or into the dark because you are mad at it.

The first time you feel a gun kick in your hand, something shifts. It vibrates up your arm and hums through your ribs. You tell yourself you never have to back down again. Knives, fists, dice, it does not matter. You think you are the same as the next man now. What you do not think about are consequences, or where a bullet travels after it leaves your barrel. Thank God none of those rounds crossed the wrong space and hit a stranger. After that, we were not going back to pretending we were harmless.

We were already stealing small things. The day came when we decided to up the anty.. In December of 1987, we went to the mall and stuck up a few people. It was sloppy and stupid. As we drove off, we counted what we had risked our lives for; what we had traumatized and terrorized our victims for: $51.00.

CHAPTER 7

JUST PLEAD GUILTY

The blue lights washed the seats. I sat in the back of the patrol car and told myself it was nothing. Intake was paperwork. Booking would be a yawn. I was a juvenile who slipped, and I would be back outside by the weekend. That was the story I sold myself while the camera flashed and the ink rolled my fingers black.

In the holding cell the other boys stared at the floor or prayed into their sleeves. I leaned back and acted like I was bored. When the guard asked about a phone call, I shook my head. I told myself I was tough. I told myself I would not give anyone the satisfaction of hearing me ask for help, but really, I was ashamed to call my mother and hear her broken heart through the speaker.

Two days passed. Two days of sitting on a steel toilet doing my business in front of strangers. Two days of trying to sleep under a bright in a cold cell under a bright light never went off. I finally called Mama. Her breath hitched when she heard my voice.

"Where are you," she asked.

"Downtown," I said.

"For what?"

"Armed robbery," I said, like I was reading a grocery list.

Silence filled the line. That's the painful silence I didn't want to hear.

***

If you have ever watched a prison program on TV such as *Lock Up Raw*, you see inmates cleaning up or shiny waxed floors. But what the camera can not relay to the watcher is the overwhelming smell of shit, piss, sweat, and fear, and death all rolled into one smell. And it's a smell no one can put into words.

You just have to smell it to know what I'm talking about. And no matter how often they finally book me in and log me in, I did not want a phone call.

I was escorted up to a cell. After the sound of the last echo from the last steel wire closing, slowly reality started to set in.

I stood there for a moment taking in my surroundings of what was my cell. It was cold outside so it felt twice as cold inside that little cell. I sat down on my bunk and slowly and silently tears started to run down my face.

Somehow I must have managed to fall asleep on that cold piece of steel, waiting on them to bring me a mattress, pillow and sheets because a sound was shutting my door for block.

Asked me did I want coffee. I turned him down, finished my tray of cold food, used the bathroom, and laid back down. It was Christmas Eve. I was in jail. And to my knowledge no one knew where I was.

That was wrong because an hour later they came to get me. I thought I was going to see the detective, but when I walked through the door and into the room, there sat my mother. I could tell she had been crying.

As I sat down she looked at me and asked one four-word simple question:

"Just tell me why."

Even after all these years I have not been fully able to answer that question.

Her next question to me was about a lawyer. I learned that one of the boys I had gotten arrested with, called his grandmother to tell her he was in jail. She in turn called my mother. Even after all that I had put my mother through at that time and would continue to put her through, she had never made me feel anything but love and worry, completely as her son.

The lawyer who charged my mother $5,000 did nothing. Absolutely nothing. I probably would have come out better going with a court-appointed lawyer than the lawyer I had. He lawyer came to see me twice. The first time he asked me, "Did you do it?" I told him yes. A few months later he came to see me the day before court and told me, "Tomorrow just plead guilty."

Only my mother was led to believe by my lawyer that I was getting out, and coming home.

CHAPTER 8

11 YEARS AND 84 DAYS

They chained us together at the wrists and ankles for court. The hallway smelled like bleach and coffee. I kept my head up and my mouth set. In my mind it was still a small thing. I had seventeen dollars in my pocket when they caught me. How bad could it be?

The courtroom looked smaller than on TV. My attorney was a thin man with tired eyes and a file that did not look thick enough to hold my future. Mama slid into the second row. She nodded once. Her internal war of shame yet support shrouded her face. I stared at the table and chewed the inside of my cheek.

"All rise."

The judge took the bench. He read names. He read charges. He did not blink much. When he said mine, the sound of it hit me low in the stomach.

"State versus David Spicer," the clerk said.

"Present," my lawyer answered.

The prosecutor stood. "Your Honor, the State is prepared to proceed," she said. "The defendant and two accomplices approached three individuals at the mall and, while armed, demanded property. He was apprehended shortly after with the weapons and proceeds."

My lawyer cleared his throat. "Your Honor, my client is seventeen. He has family support. He is enrolled in school. This is a noninjury case. We ask the court to consider leniency and rehabilitation over incarceration."

The prosecutor shook her head. "Three separate victims, Your Honor. A firearm was displayed. He may be seventeen, but this was an adult crime."

The judge turned to me. "Mr. Spicer, do you understand the charges."

"Yes, sir."

"Do you have anything you wish to say before I pronounce sentence."

I looked at Mama. Her hands were folded so tight her knuckles were pale. I felt heat rise in my neck and decided to play it cool.

"I made a mistake," I said. "I'm sorry. I promise It will not happen again."

The judge watched me a beat too long. "Is that all."

I shrugged. "Yes, sir."

He nodded as if that confirmed something he already knew. "Stand."

We stood.

"This court has considered your age, your record, the facts of the case, and the statements of counsel," he said. "You want me to believe this is small. It is not small. You carried a gun into a public place. You pointed it at three people. That is not small."

My jaw tightened, but I kept my face blank.

He continued, "You think you are untouchable because you are seventeen. You are not. In this courtroom, your choices have weight."

He glanced at my lawyer, then at the prosecutor, then back at me. "For armed robbery with a deadly weapon, I sentence you to 50 years with 44 years to be suspended and 6 years to serve. In addition, five years to be served consecutively, plus time served.

The words did not land at first. It was like a dream. When I woke, the number hit like a ton of bricks. Eleven years and eighty-four days. It sounded like a math problem from someone else's life.

"No," I said before I could stop myself.

The bailiff took a step.

My lawyer tugged my sleeve. "Do not," he whispered.

I turned toward Mama. Her mouth pressed thin. A tear slid, and she wiped it away like it was sweat. She did not stand or shout. She did not beg. She had done all that already, in prayers I never heard.

"Mr. Spicer," the judge said, voice even, "you will be remanded today. You will be credited for time served."

"Your Honor," my lawyer tried, "if the court would consider—"

"Denied," the judge said. "Next matter."

The gavel sounded like a door slamming at the end of a long hall. The bailiff touched my elbow. Chains kissed the floor as we turned.

"Mama," I said.

She stood. "Son," she answered.

"I am sorry."

"I know," she said.

They led me through a side door. The hallway was colder than the courtroom. Fluorescent buzz sat in my ears. My legs felt hollow, like they might fold. I did not fall. I stared at the cinder blocks, counted the lines in the mortar, and tried to swallow the number.

"Eleven years and eighty-four days."

I had told myself it was nothing. I had told myself I was slick. I had told myself I would be home by the weekend. I thought of the mall, the blue lights, my arrogance. I thought of Mama's hands. The judges words echoed in my mind, "This is not small."

On the ride out, the bus windows were scratched and cloudy. We passed the field where we ran sprints until our ribs burned. We passed the corner store where I bought sodas for my brothers. I watched the houses slide by and understood, finally, that consequences are not a story someone tells you. They are a door you walk through and a life that keeps going without you until you find a way to walk back.

The inmate I was chained to looked over at me.

"What you get?" he asked.

I looked straight ahead and mustered the only words I could...

"Time."

CHAPTER 9

WELCOME TO PARCHMAN PENITENTIARY

Everything before court moves slow. County time drags. You wait weeks, sometimes months, listening to war stories and Hollywood guesses about prison. Then the judge says the number, and the gears jump. They want you off their books and gone. Walking out of county feels like leaving your own funeral, except you are alive enough to feel every bit of it.

In my head I could still hear my mother: "Everything is going to be okay. Do not forget to pray."

It is strange that the same kind of bus that takes kids to school takes inmates to prison. Bars on the windows, same hard seats, same rattling glass. We rolled north on Highway 49 into the Delta, B. B. King country and Muddy Waters. Parchman was about to be home for the next few years.

Two hours on that road gives you time to think and time to pray. You can usually spot the men who have done time before. They talk, joke, and trade names. The ones who have not are quiet and counting breaths. Quiet and nervous can save your life.

The prison came into view like a rumor made of concrete. Razor wire stitched the sky. Someone on the bus said, "This is it." The heat rushed us when the door swung open. Intake was summer air with no air-conditioning. In winter they promised heat, but nobody walked around in short sleeves.

Back then Camp 15 took the new bodies. Every building had a number and a reputation. Camp 5 had one I learned to hate. The bus stopped at Red by 15 and men crowded the fence. Some yelled, "Fresh meat." Some just looked hard, eyes moving like they were reading a list and hoping to see a name they knew. If you were lucky, a homeboy on the yard sent word you were straight, which bought you a little time to find your feet.

They called my name. "Spicer."

I stepped forward, gave my number—65707—and walked through the gate. A couple of older brothers I knew from county nodded me in. They pressed steel into my palm like it was a toothbrush. Then the lay of the land: who ran dope, who made wine, who could fix a problem, who would be your problem, who to speak to, who to leave alone.

The dorm was one long breath of heat and noise. Ten open toilets in a row. No stalls. Showers with no doors and no curtains. Privacy did not live here. County gave you corners. Parchman gave you a crowd and a choice. You either learned to move with your shoulders squared and your eyes awake, or you let the place choose for you.

This is the part people do not say out loud. The first days, men watch. They watch how you stand in line, whether you hold a stare, whether you drop it, whether you flinch when someone brushes past you. Reputation is currency. Silence can be read as respect or as weakness, and you do not get to decide which. People test boundaries. The test is the point. If you shrink, you get marked. If you answer wrong, you get marked a different way. There is no tutorial. There is only how you carry yourself and what that tells the room.

The guards at Red did not waste breath on speeches. If you were passing through, the lesson was simple. Learn fast, or the stretcher would teach you. Word traveled faster than the fans. Debts mattered. Promises mattered. Names mattered. Talking on another man's case did not. You kept your area tight, kept your mouth measured, paid what you owed when you said you would, and kept your eyes up without turning it into a challenge.

I found my rack and sat. The room was metal clanks, low talk, and the wet echo of showers. A dice game started in a corner. Somebody argued simple and quiet, like they had argued it a hundred times before. On the far side of the dorm two men moved together the way people do when they have carved out a corner of this world and called it theirs. I stared at the ceiling and felt a hard, tired hate rise in me for where my life had landed.

Then I heard my mother again. "Son, do not forget to pray."

So I prayed. I slid back on the thin mattress, tucked my hand under the blanket, and let the prayer hold me while the dorm kept breathing. Somewhere a fan turned slow. Keys rang against a belt. A man laughed, short and sharp. Another cursed under his breath. I watched the seams in the cinder block until my eyes burned, and finally sleep took me, not because I felt safe, but because my body shut down and God gave me a small mercy.

CHAPTER 10

FROM R&O TO GLADIATOR SCHOOL: CAMP 29, "CASTLE GREY SKULL"

When you see a man come out of prison carved up with muscle, do not assume he fell in love with salads and eight hours of sleep. Most of us work out so we can handle ourselves when it turns physical. Readiness is not a hobby. It is survival.

There are lines you cannot let anyone cross. If a man disrespects your space, breathes on your locker like he owns it, or takes from your store or your clothes, he is testing you and your next months. In prison some words are not just insults. "Punk," "bitch," "snitch," "rat," "Chester." Say one of those to a man and the room looks at what happens next. If you walk from every challenge, a label sticks, and labeled men become targets. Targets get fed on.

The lane you want is simple. Be the stand-up convict who pays debts on time, stays clean, keeps business quiet, and avoids the police. Do not try to play champion. The louder you posture, the more often someone will step up to see if you mean it. Size does not save you. Consistency does.

An old head told me, "A man who is ready does not have to get ready. I would rather the police catch me prepared than another inmate catch me unprepared." That is the concrete talking. From then on I carried protection, because the law behind the wire has its own rules and it does not grant exceptions to anyone.

Six months into my bid, somebody decided to test that. But first, understand the yard. Camp 29 had a name. Folks called it "Castle Grey Skull," half joke, half warning, from that old He-Man cartoon. The front of the unit looked like rock. Life there was asphalt, concrete, and steel. If you wanted into the farm lines to pick or chop—cotton, peas, beans, potatoes, corn—you passed through 29.

Parchman fed us from the same ground. Beans. Powdered eggs. Soy patties. On holidays, maybe fried eggs and real sausage. Chicken or fish showed up about as often as a snowstorm. If you had thirty dollars on your books, commissary filled in the blanks, which is why men stopped complaining when money flowed.

Respect is a currency too. You spend it or save it over little things that somehow matter in here: a seat you always use in the kitchen, a foul that was too hard on the court, a place in line. From the outside it sounds petty. On the inside it is pressure. This is a different planet with its own gravity. You stay mentally, physically, and spiritually awake, twenty-four seven. Recreation is rare. Sleep requires trust.

I loved basketball. I could play. We ran five-on-five with cases of soda on the line. Lose, you pay five cases. At first it was clean. Then it got personal. Every time I took the lane, my defender did more than foul. He tried to put me down. I returned the favor.

One game I decided I was finished with cat and mouse. I baited him, sold a fake, and put him down hard. He hit the floor. I followed with enough heat to make the point until hands pulled me off and the cuffs clicked. That ended that matchup. The yard took its lesson.

When violence erupts, the dorm freezes. Men watch to learn who can handle himself and where the cracks might be. That day said what it needed to say. I was not volunteering to be managed. I was not looking to run wild either. I am a big man, but out on the street I pray I would have walked away. In here, civilization is thin. When someone is down, too many keep going because they are sure that is what would be done to them. If you do not make an impact, you might not get a second chance to breathe. Send the message now, or pay for it later.

That was the economy. Men bet on fights like weather forecasts. When a batch of wine hit the dorm, tempers rose and odds changed. Paranoia ran on high octane. I was lucky more than once. I was blessed more than once. I believe the prayers my grandmother sent up before I was born kept finding me even here. I had a few close calls. I was stabbed once in eleven years. I took the scar and the lesson.

Around twenty-five or twenty-six, a switch flipped. I could see the door to freedom in the distance. A couple of years, if I kept my head. I started to move different. In prison you rarely stay put. Units change. Camps change. Faces change. You meet every kind of man and hear every kind of story. Age teaches you that not every look is a reason to fight and not every bump is a challenge to your soul.

A scholar could make a chart of how much ex-cons move after release. When freedom comes back, staying still feels like wearing the wrong size shoes. Parchman is twenty-three thousand acres of flat farmland and a clock that ticks in slow motion. For almost nine years my thoughts were simple: stay alive, stay ready, wake up tomorrow.

People on the outside ask why every inmate does not come out with a trade or a degree. The truth is that building a future is hard when you are surrounded by present-tense danger. Hate is a bad teacher but stress is a worse one. I entered at seventeen thinking I would be out in a couple of years and pick up where I left off. Then I realized I was still young, still healthy, and the prime years for becoming a man were being spent on another curriculum: life versus death, sanity versus madness.

The lesson prison teaches best is "do unto others before they do unto you." I learned it. I learned too well. If the lesson was supposed to be rehabilitation, I failed that course with color. The place taught me more underground than any classroom taught me above it.

Even so, I set my mind to get out, find a job and build a life. I refused to let my first mistakes write my whole story. I told myself that on loops, then reality answered back.

CHAPTER 11

FREE AT LAST, FREE AT LAST, THANK GOD ALMIGHTY, I'M FREE AT LAST.

Sunday, December 27, 1998

I had not slept in two days. The bunk felt like a trap that would snap shut if I let my eyes close. Part of me was scared the nightmare would spool right back up. Part of me was scared I would not wake up at all. Six months from my date I started telling my case manager, "I am getting out." He would nod, look at the screen, tap a key, and say, "I know." Everybody is in that computer. Your count, your work, your write-ups, your out date. Still, it is different when the words come out of your own mouth. Saying it made it feel like I could tug the future an inch closer.

The real sign came ten days from the door. They called my name at the window. A man slid a form under the glass and pointed to a line. I signed. That was my check. The State of Mississippi and Uncle Sam saying thank you for eleven years of service. Service like cotton picked in heat that makes your eyes sting. Service like fields and kitchens and clocks that moved only when they wanted to. The amount read: one hundred dollars and one cent. Gate money. We had another name for it that tasted like rust. It was just enough to get mad. Just enough to get stuck.

I thought about the men who would walk out with nothing but a handshake and that check. No mother waiting. No cousin with a couch. No brothers with a tank full of gas. Even back then, the cheapest motel chewed up thirty dollars a night, no questions asked, no refunds. A sandwich and a bus ride and you were broke by afternoon. We talk about why people come back like it is a riddle. It is not a riddle. You put a man on ice for a decade and then hand him a bill, not a bridge, and ask why his feet stay cold.

They asked whether someone was coming for me or if I needed a bus ticket. I signed what they put down and kept my voice light. The system had planned enough of my life. God would plan the rest. My mother had already prayed the road open. I believed that then. I still do.

People on the outside like to think you walk out, take a deep breath, and close that chapter like a book you can shelve. Maybe you could if the world did not keep reminding you what you have been. The gate clanged and there were my brothers, taller, broader, with the faces of the boys I left still hiding in the edges of their smiles. Back when I went in they were little. Now they were men with jobs and keys and jokes of their own.

We did not go far before I wanted to stop. A gas station. The kind of place that sells a hundred versions of the same sugar. I walked down an aisle slow, not because I did not know what I wanted, but because there were too many choices and I had not had choices in so long. I picked up gum. Eleven years without it because you cannot have anything soft on the tier. I tore the silver open, slid a stick in my mouth, and put my feet on the dash like a teenager who had borrowed his mama's car. The first pop of sweetness felt like a parade marching back down my tongue. I did not mean to smile as big as I did.

"If gum got you grinning like that," one brother said, "wait until you smell a woman."

All of us laughed. I kept chewing. I chewed like I wanted to use up the whole day.

Driving through town was like watching a movie made from pieces of my memory spliced with scenes I had never seen. New buildings where grass used to wave. Fresh paint over bricks that had been peeling before I left. Empty lots turned into stores that sold shoes too clean to wear on any street I knew. Some old signs still hanging where the money ran out, the ghosts of businesses that had not made it. I pressed my palm to the glass the way a kid does when he wants to be sure the world is real. The glass felt cool and steady under my hand. The future felt like something I could smudge with a fingerprint.

At my mother's table that first week I ate slow, not because I did not like the food, but because my head and my hands were not on the same clock. In there, they hand you one utensil and expect it to last the whole bid. Lose it, and you are out of luck until you hustle another. You learn to keep it on you. Shoe, pocket, rolled in a sock, under your pillow. That habit rode home with me like a passenger I could not shake. I caught myself slipping the fork toward my waistband without thinking, like the kitchen police might raid the drawer. I set it back down and made myself leave it there. That is what programming feels like. You do not ask for it. It arrives and installs itself behind your eyes.

Everything was like that. Second nature. Sit with your back to a wall where you can see the door. Count exits. Scan a room without staring. Put your shoes where your toes can find them in the dark. In there, every second of the day is spoken for by a rule, a count, a bell, a name. Out here the rules are quiet. The freedom is loud. You have to reprogram your head while your body keeps doing what it was trained to do for years. Hollywood makes that look pretty. It is not pretty. It is work.

A few days in I felt the weight of my family's eyes. It was not mean. It was curiosity. Civilians learning who had come back in the place of the boy who left. Little cousins— now grown—stood in the doorway and watched me tie my shoes like it was a trick. "Unc," one of them said, "you want more tea." I nodded and smiled and tried to map names to faces. In the corner a baby cried. I did the math and realized I was an uncle almost ten times over. Time had gone and built a whole neighborhood while I was counting the same cinder blocks.

You cannot help but compare prices in your head. More than thirty thousand dollars a year to cage me. More than forty thousand for some colleges to let a kid sit in a lecture hall and try to shape a life. We chose the warehouse. We chose it again and again. Then we crossed our arms and asked why the shelves keep filling up. We talk about rehabilitation like it is a class you can enroll a man in. The truth is uglier and simpler. If you lock a boy up five years or more, he will learn fifty ways to make money wrong before he learns five ways to make money right. You can be mad at that truth. I have been mad at it myself. It is still the truth.

Years later, after the welcome-home plates and the first jobs and the first stumbles, me and my baby brother got into it. Not over anything worth keeping. Voices got tight. He squared his shoulders because he was a man now, and I felt the old reflex stand up in my chest like it wanted to be counted. In that moment I had a choice. I handed my mother the spare key I had made, told her I would be back tomorrow for my clothes, and walked out. The air outside felt like a test I had passed by the skin of my teeth. Freedom is not just a gate swinging open. It is a choice you make on a Tuesday when your blood is hot and your hands remember another language.

That first night back, I lay under a ceiling that did not belong to the state and counted the slow blink of sleep coming on. My brothers' laughter from the ride still sat in the room like a bright thing. My mother's voice from all those letters still stood by the bed.

"Do not forget," she would write at the bottom, every time.

"I will not," I told the dark.

Morning came in thin and gold under the blinds. The world was the same and not the same. The gum wrapper was still on the dresser where I had left it, folded into a tiny square like a promise. I picked it up and slid it into my pocket. Small, yes. Silly to someone else, maybe. To me it was proof.

People say, "You must feel free." I did. I felt wobbly too, like a man who just stepped off a rocking boat onto a steady dock and could still feel the waves in his ankles. Freedom takes practice. It takes time. It takes patience from the people who love you, and it takes patience you did not know you had for yourself.

The day stretched out ahead, wide as a road that finally ran past the fence line. The check was folded in my wallet. The gum sat sweet on my tongue. My mother hummed in the kitchen. Somewhere outside a car backfired and I did not flinch. I breathed in. I breathed out. I started, slow and stubborn, to learn what staying free might look like, one ordinary moment at a time.

CHAPTER 12

ON MY OWN AND UNPREPARED

Grown folks talk about bills like weights tied to their ankles. Rent. Lights. Groceries. Insurance. All those etceteras that stack and lean. When I was young I swore I would sprint past all that and prove it was easy. That is how youth works. You think gravity is for other people.

I peeled three hundred dollars from what I had and handed it to a landlord who did not ask questions I could not answer. A three hundred dollar room, no deposit, no first and last month rent due. The neighborhood wore its rough like a coat that had seen too many winters. Around there you did not need a judge to get evicted. Miss rent and the warning lived in the landlord's eyes. If that did not move you, there were other ways. The apartment was bare as a fist, walls scuffed to the color of old bones, but the key turned and the door opened and the space was mine. That mattered more than paint.

January 1999. Cold slid under the window and pooled on the floor. No bed. No couch. I folded a hoodie for a pillow, spread a jacket like a thin blanket, and lay on hardwood that answered my heartbeat. The streetlight outside laid a rectangle of pale orange on the wall, and I told myself this was the start of a big city life even if the city did not know my name.

Getting the power turned on in my name felt like ceremony. I stood there, palm on the switch, and clicked a tired bulb awake. That hum said, You are here. I had a few bills already and no cushion. Luck and blessing held my elbows like two steady hands.

Work was the next mountain. Most men walking out, ninety nine out of a hundred, truly want right at first. A job is a job if it keeps the lights paying attention. The trouble is your feet if you do not have a car. I did not know the buses. Did not know which line crossed which avenue, or that you had to pull a cord to make the driver stop. I learned by watching my stop drift by the window, three blocks back, while my jaw tightened. I got off angry, walked it off, and climbed on the next one wiser.

Applications hit different. "List your last three jobs." "Supervisor name." "Reason for leaving." "Phone number for verification." Fluorescent lights buzzed over my head like impatient bees. I bent over the form and felt small. My pen hovered over blank spaces that wanted a life I did not have on paper.

Warehouse work made sense. Big bodies with good attitudes get hired faster than fancy résumés in the right kind of place. That was the pep talk. The truth was I wanted somewhere that valued showing up on time and lifting right over charm I did not own yet.

I ducked into a Burger King, bought a cheap meal, and slid into a booth where the heater worked. The window faced a shuttered tire shop with a cracked sign still bolted to the brick. Dust filmed the glass. A single weed grew through a split in the asphalt like a hand raised in a tired classroom. My mind, trained by years to hunt angles, started to hum.

The thought came fast. Cut a corner. Paper over the blanks. The old life whistled sweet, promising quick doors opening without keys. I felt the pull and the price in the same breath. I called my brother in Arkansas, told him I was broke and tired and asked if he would vouch for my character if somebody called. He said yes. Then he asked if I had a phone. I laughed and said no. I went to the mall and bought a pager, the poor man's voicemail. Holding that little black rectangle felt like holding a rope.

From the mall I walked to the county office and applied for food stamps. The woman behind the glass spoke plain, no sweetening. She told me what would come, when it would come, and to check back in three months if I still needed help. I nodded. Pride balanced on my tongue like a coin I did not want to spend. I told myself I would not be back.

Nights stretched long in that apartment. Pipes knocked messages in the walls. Sirens practiced scales a few blocks over. I ate cross-legged on the floor and counted the budget out loud. Bus fare. A little food. Maybe a cheap pair of work gloves if a warehouse said yes. I wrote lists on the backs of envelopes and cereal box flaps, then lost them and started again.

People do not tell you how loud temptation gets when the room is quiet. I had been out a couple of weeks. Every time something went left, I could feel the old life lean over my shoulder and breathe. Fast money talks smooth. "One day to get right. One night to take the edge off." It leaves out the cuffs and the numbers. I told myself the truth, then told it again, until the voice got tired of hearing me.

The buses got easier. I learned which drivers would answer a question and which ones could not be bothered. I learned the rhythm of the doors, how to plant my feet when the light turned yellow. The morning regulars became landmarks. A woman with a lunch pail and a Bible that she opened to the same page every day. A man in paint-splattered jeans who could sleep sitting up and still wake for his stop without looking. They did not know me, but being part of their pattern felt like proof I was trying.

Applications did not get friendlier, but my hand got steadier. Where it asked for supervisors I listed the last men who spoke to me with respect behind the wire, men who had seen me work and would say so. Where it asked for reason for leaving I wrote, "Completed term." Where it asked for skills

I told the truth. I can lift. I can arrive early. I can stay late. I learn fast. The rest you can teach.

At night I folded my clothes for tomorrow and laid them by the spot on the floor where I slept. Shoes by the door, laces open. I sat with my back to the wall because habit and comfort had braided together. Before I stood up, I whispered a thank you to God. Then I went out and tried again.

Small things began to stack. A driver who nodded when I got on. A clerk who said, "You missed a line, right there," and slid the application back without attitude. A stranger who held the bus when he saw me jog the last ten steps. None of it was headline news. All of it felt like bricks.

On a Tuesday the pager buzzed. The vibration in my pocket felt like a bird trapped under my hand.

"Can you be here by seven," the voice asked when I found a pay phone and called back.

"Yes, sir," I said, barefoot in my kitchen, toes cold on the tile. "I can be there by six-thirty."

I hung up and leaned my head against the cabinet. Outside, a siren wound down into calm. Inside, the bulb hummed and the room seemed to breathe with me. I set out my clothes, set my shoes, set my alarm, and sat a while longer, letting the quiet be a kind of music.

Morning would come, and with it another chance to build something that could hold my weight. I was not ready for everything. I was ready enough.

CHAPTER 13

MAKING AN HONEST LIVING

On the ride back to my apartment I bought a newspaper from a box with a cloudy window. No car meant jobs had to live on a bus line, so the classifieds were my map. At home I sat cross-legged on the floor and circled anything that sounded like "possible" instead of "dream." Night came on. I showered, ate Ramen from a chipped bowl, and stretched out on the hardwood. Sleep found me and left before the sun did.

Morning, early. I fed coins into a pay phone and called my brother for those references he promised. He read me names and addresses, then said, "I will pick up if anyone calls. You good."

"I am trying to be," I said.

About the tenth call, a security company told me to come in right away. "Interview today," the woman said. "Guy quit last night. We need a body."

The office smelled like copier toner and burnt coffee. The manager wore a short-sleeve shirt and a tired tie. He skimmed my application, looked at my size, nodded. "Site is an apartment complex. Walk the halls, keep a presence, check doors and lots. The point is peace of mind for residents." He glanced at the clock. "Can you start tonight."

"Yes, sir."

"Be here at six for training."

I showed up at 5:45. They handed me a polo with SECURITY stitched over the pocket. The veteran who trained me had socks that did not match and eyes that said he had been doing doubles. We walked and talked for hours. Keys. Rounds. Radios. How to write an incident the way bosses like it. He watched me do the loop twice, then took the lead and ran it again. "You will be fine," he said. "Shift is six to six. Seven days."

It sounded heavy, but work is work. Then came the catch. "High post," he said. "You have to carry."

I nodded, but my stomach tightened. Back at the apartment I lay on the floor and stared at the ceiling. Sleep did not come. By eight in the morning I had made my decision. I walked back to the office and told the manager the truth I could live with.

"I want this job," I said. "I will be good at it. But I cannot wear a gun. When I was young, I watched my father take his own life with one, and I have a problem being around them."

He went quiet. Papers clicked under his palm. He looked up and saw I meant it. "You still have the job," he said. "We will place you at a no-carry site. Be on time."

That night I worked my first twelve. The rounds felt like a test I was passing with each door I checked. When the shift ended I signed out with a smile so wide it surprised me. Twenty-four hours awake and I was not even tired. I had earned an honest dollar. The day looked different, almost brighter.

Life stayed simple because it had to. Groceries, then home. No TV. No radio. No game system. Not even a phone yet. A few months in, the guard who trained me said there was a posting at a furniture warehouse paying day hours. "Eight to four," he said. "You want it."

"I want both," I said. "I will make it work."

I pictured a stack of paychecks growing into a used car, a couch, some clothes that did not come from the bottom shelf. Maybe a date that did not end with me counting quarters. Nights I walked rounds. Days I assembled furniture and rode shotgun on deliveries. I told myself I could grab an hour of sleep here and there, like a thief stealing time.

A few weeks later, trouble showed up at the security post. A car up on blocks. Tires gone. I followed procedure and phoned it in. The officer arrived twenty-three minutes later, wrote, shrugged, drove away. The manager pulled me into the office. "If you had been armed," he said, "you could have stopped it." He slid a check across the desk. Terminated. The word landed like a brick.

I walked to the bank and cashed out what they owed me. The teller said, "Have a nice day," the way people say it when they have no idea what your day holds. I called the warehouse and told them I was sick. I did not want to lift anything but the weight in my chest. I bought beer and a bag and tried to sleep my anger off, but anger does not sleep. It paces.

By morning the shame tasted like battery acid. I called the warehouse again and told them I quit. I told my brother I was heading to Arkansas, but I was not going anywhere. I was tired of doing right and watching the wrong wind blow my little pile of cards off the table. The old life whistled from the alley.

A thought marched in, fast and ugly. Buy a piece. Rob banks. Make the world pay me back.

I stood in the middle of the apartment that was still more echo than home and stared at the door. My hand rose toward the knob like it belonged to someone else.

A siren wailed somewhere close, then far. The refrigerator clicked and hummed. I felt my mother's voice in my chest the way you feel thunder through a wall.

"Son," she said in that voice I had heard a thousand times, "do not forget."

I froze with my fingers on the brass, breathing like I had run a mile.

The hallway outside was quiet as a held breath.

CHAPTER 14

THE BANK

It is wild what your mind drags up when you are drunk. Anyone who has been around a drunk knows you usually get one of two kinds: the soft, happy kind or the hard, mean kind. Coming down, I was groggy and angry. My pity party rolled back through my whole life. I thought about prison and decided there was no such thing as justice. I told myself I would not keep struggling to do right if the deck was fixed. If I was going back, I would not go back for something petty.

So I chose the biggest wrong I could think of. I told myself I was going to rob a bank.

The plan came together fast in that ugly way bad ideas do when pride is driving. I decided I needed a gun. I told myself I would never use it, that a note would be enough.

"You get less time that way and less money."

All I knew from years of hearing other convicts was that if you found a bank with FDIC on the door, that bank was just right. The money was insured and all the tellers were trained to do what you say.

I fed myself more lies, the kind you hear passed around on tiers and in yards, the kind that make crime sound like math.

I walked into the first place I chose and scanned to see how many people working there, how busy they were, but most importantly if they had a security guard. Everything looked good. So I left, walked across the street to a hardware store, bought a dog rope to hold the gun between my pants and a hoodie to hide from the police. Shows you how little I thought.

The air felt too bright. My heartbeat ticked in my ears. I told myself I was not a hero and did not want to play one. I did not want to hurt anyone. I just wanted the money and a way out of the hole.

I stepped to the counter. I let the metal show. I said the words everyone knows.

"This is a robbery."

Eyes went wide. Hands moved. A bag appeared and bills started dropping. One teller moved slow, feeding singles like she was trying to buy time. Panic climbed my throat. I made a terrible choice and fired a shot in the ceiling.

The blast in that small room felt like a tank had cracked the ceiling. People screamed. Everybody moved faster. I kept glancing at nothing and everything, lungs burning, heart hammering. The world squeezed down to hands, bills, breath.

I kept looking at my watch, and when one minute was up, I grabbed the bags and ran for the door.

When the adrenaline burned off, I was alone in with more money than I had ever touched in my life. Seventeen thousand dollars. The best part of it was tax free. I had stolen from Uncle Sam instead of rich stealing from me.

That number looked impossible lying there. It was more than anyone I knew back home would see at once from clocking a nine-to-five for months. No taxes. No forms. Just cash and a pounding in my skull.

That should have been the part where I came to my senses. It was not. The rush felt like standing on a rooftop with the wind under my ribs. For a few wild minutes I believed I had beaten something that could not be beaten. I felt like Superman

I took that $17,000 and pointed myself at New Orleans. I was going to party like a rock star. That is exactly what I did. Hundreds dropped for tips. Smoke curling before noon. Drinks stacked by midnight. The city breathed hot and electric, brass leaking out of doorways, laughter lifting off the sidewalk like steam. From wake-up to crash I floated on cloud one thousand. Prices did not matter. What a woman charged did not matter. Hotel rates did not matter. In my head the math was simple. When I ran out, I would refill.

Easy come, easy go.

When you are twenty-two, raised poor, with the years from seventeen to twenty-eight eaten by a number and a gate, seventeen thousand feels like proof that rich is a feeling and it finally found you. It lasted days.

I had a few dollars left, so I headed back to Mississippi, telling myself I would cool off on the Gulf Coast. The water felt like a clean slate. The party followed me anyway. One night bled into the next, faces swapping out while music alcohol and drugs stayed the same. With liquor on top of weed and powder whispering in my ear, my body lied and said it could not feel a thing. I knew better. I kept going.

I needed a new roll. Jackson tugged at me because I knew its corners and it knew my steps. Familiar can be a trap, but I was beyond that kind of wisdom. Family had no idea what I was doing. I told myself I wanted to lay eyes on them. Looking back, I was also saying a crooked kind of goodbye. In my mind, getting caught meant ten to twenty. I told myself I could not do that much time. Then I told myself I would if I had to. Denial and pride holding hands.

I knew my way around and I was comfortable robbing banks there. The chances of someone seeing and recognizing my photo on the news was very good, but at that point I simply no longer cared. I knew almost all the banks by my heart. Plus I wanted to see some of my family who had no idea I was robbing banks.

I went to visit my mother and then drove around looking at different banks. I dad driving routes to see how much time it took me to get to the highway, because I knew if I made it to the highway, my chances of getting away was good.

I found two banks that I was comfortable with. I sat in my car across from the bank smoking a cigarette and scoping the outside. It felt good. I had to go inside to see if they had a security guard.

I drove a couple blocks away from the bank, parked my car, and walked back to the bank. When I walked inside there were no customers and only two tellers. It was perfect.

I walked behind the teller counter, pulled my weapon, yelled, "This is a robbery," and passed them each a bag.

"Load em up! No alarms."

Out of the blue, one teller dumped all the money she had put into the bag out onto the floor.

"What the fuck are you doing?" I screamed. Was she trying to be a hero?

"I'm getting the dye pack out."

I couldn't believe it. Was she helping me? I went over and started helping them put money back in the bag off the floor. Imagine it: a bank robber and bank tellers working together like a team. I looked at my watch, and 60 seconds was up. I grabbed both bags and left. I got away with $7,000.

Side note: I later found out the banked claimed $10,000. So one of those bank tellers or manager must have taken $3,000 for themselves and claimed $10,000 for insurance. For 60 seconds of sin, I was 7,000 richer. I held more money than some folks I love would see at once from months of clocking in. I rolled onto the highway under a sky so clean it felt like a trick. I smoked and grinned like the horizon was smiling back.

The second pile vanished faster than the first. Hotels that smelled like bleach and lemon. Trays I could not afford. Hands that took and took. Hundred dollar tips left on tables like I had money to bless.

Paranoia climbed in the passenger seat and buckled up. I checked into one place and left fifteen minutes later. I slept in my clothes because I did not trust sleep. I bought another gun for no reason but the story I was telling myself. I was not Jesse James, just a tired man with a pocket full of fire and no plan for the burn.

Remorse started visiting at odd angles. On a balcony at dawn. In a quiet hallway where a baby cried behind a door. Between songs when the DJ took a breath. I thought about turning myself in. I thought about running until the map ran out. I thought about daring the world to catch me. The last thought won.

I swore I would not touch anything close to the beach. The road there was too narrow, the distance too unforgiving. Saying the rule out loud felt wise. Then I broke it. A small bank sat on the shoulder of the highway like a brick with a flag. I told myself I would only look.

Before that I swept through Hattiesburg. A college town's noise could hide my storm. There were bank branches on top of branches, some close enough to wave across the gap, but glass stood where I did not want it and presence showed up where I did not need it. I left empty-handed and hungry. On the way back, the little highway bank stared me down.

I went and found a girl to be my get away driver. I went back and did it. Twenty-eight hundred. Shame and relief rode the same breath. I stepped into sunlight that felt like it had teeth and managed to get away.

The cash sat heavy in my pocket, like it knew more about the future than I did.

I knew the car was now a flare in the night, numbers and routes just waiting to be connected by the feds, so I found a pay phone and called a cab. It rolled up with the windows down and the radio low.

"Where to," the driver asked.

"New Orleans."

Part of me was ready for this party to be over.

So many times I just wanted to be like Dorothy in *The Wizard of Oz* — I could click my heels together three times, wake up back home, and find out it was all a dream — or was.

On the way from Gulfport, the cab driver asked me what I did for a living.

I lifted my shirt, showing him my two guns,

"I robbed banks."

He laughed, believing I was joking.

"I'm serious. I just robbed one when you picked me up."

I laughed to ease his mind. Besides, I didn't want him to feel like he was in danger. The driver was really cool, so when he dropped me off in New Orleans I paid him $100 for the trip.

"Let me get your number," I said. "When I need to come go back to Gulfport, I'll call you to come get me.".

When the cab driver got back to Gulfport, he saw my face on the news show I was wanted for robbing banks.

Once back in the Big Easy, I wasted no time hooking back up with prostitutes and blowing through cash as if I had a printing press.

I checked into the motel on Friday night and by Monday morning I had $1.10 left.

I called the cab driver to pick me up.

He sent the FBI.

CHAPTER 15

O.P.P. JAIL

When they walked me into the Orleans Parish Prison on August 7th, 2000, a gospel song by Yolanda Adams was playing. Standing there listening to that gospel song, tears started to silently roll down my face. I was not crying so much for me, but that I had made my mother a promise that I would never go back to prison and I had broken that promise.

The old familiar smells of old, dried piss, shit, death, and fear hit me like a Mack truck, bringing me back to reality. I had to get my thug straight and quick, because I was back in the belly of the beast and someone seeing me crying could be mistaken as a sign of weakness, and that could bring the predators out for an attack.

DAVID SPICER

They fingerprinted me, took my mug shot. I took a quick shower while a guard sprayed me with some kind of chemical that was supposed to be for lice, just in case I had any. I was dressed into the blue jeans with black letters O.P.P. on the leg.

The irony: years after Naughty by Nature had everyone chanting "O.P.P." for "other people's property," I was stamped O.P.P. at Orleans Parish Prison, other people's property in the most literal way—property of the federal government.

I received my bedroll which consisted of one wool blanket that always itched whichever part of your skin it came in contact with, two sheets, a mattress that's smaller than a twin-size mattress, one roll of toilet paper, small tube of toothpaste, a half of a toothbrush, to keep you from making a shank out of it, but 24 inmates still did. I got one old towel that was actually a rag after a couple hundred boys had used to wipe God knows what before it was mine to use. In prison they tell you don't wait too damn far.

I knew I would have to hand wash myself before I used it. One bar of soap and a plastic cup and spoon that had to last me the duration of my stay. I hit the cell block. I was no longer David Spicer. I was Federal Prisoner #27226-034.

A prisoner taking that long walk to a cell is a lot like the movie *The Green Mile*. Everything seems to move so slow. The motion and the walk so long. The buzz of the electric steel wired opening and closing with big bangs and clicks let you know that they control you. You're like an animal in a zoo.

88

In many cases, that's what happens. They either make you into an animal in order to survive because if you don't become a predator, you simply become the prey. They break you by degrading you and belittling you so much until your mind, body and soul start to understand that you do not have to die to go to hell. You are already in hell.

When you tell a guard that you know your rights, they are quick to remind you with a boot up your ass or a punch to the head that in this world, you won't have any rights at all. You don't even have an identity. Just your identity as a number. And even if everything has been stripped from you, and if you allow them to take away the only thing that you have left, then they have broken you. That one thing is "hope." If you are going to have a chance at surviving, then you are immediately going to have to live by a total different set of rules.

In prison and jail, there is only one rule: there are no rules. You live or you die. It's just that simple. All's fair in love and war. This war. You do unto him before he does unto you. Hope that you lose. Even how you act as a cold-blooded killer, you either become one in your mind or you become somebody's bitch.

Sucking dicks and being fucked in your ass over and over, day and night, 365 days of the year with no one to help you. The guards are like innocent witnesses to a crime. They don't want to get involved, even though it's their job. The guards recognize this as hell. A dog eat dog world. Many of them are simply trying to make it home in one piece.

To them, it's just a job that does not pay enough, and better you than them, so be the hunter or the hunted.

Once you become cold blooded, you just can't turn a switch and go back to being normal because it just does not work that way. That's why I think people who have spent years in prison—especially violent prisons—walk out of prison and while committing their next crime, go on a killing rampage. It's hard to convince your brain that human life means much when your own had no value.

Having gone from a rough childhood to years behind bars, every day wired to danger, you learn that life can jump from zero to sixty without warning. How do you ever deprogram that. Even inside, unless you are headed to the hole, a guard walks you only to the outer door of your tier. When that steel clicks, it is God for us all. Every man for himself. You cannot call mama. You cannot call daddy. Like the military, you pray for peace and train for war.

I hit the federal side with thirty-nine other men. The door locked, and I braced to pay whatever price the room asked. I walked the range slow and met eyes one by one. In prison, men read your eyes. Drop your head and they taste fear. Hold the look, no grin, no flinch, and the message is clear. I am not here to be your friend. If it comes to it, we will go. Better judged by twelve than carried by six.

A dozen steps in, there was no pulling back. I made my rack tight and a man stepped into the cell. "I am your cellie," he said. "They just ran your picture on the news. Said you are from Mississippi, did eleven at Parchman." He had homeboys up there. I named one and described him down to the twenty gold teeth in his mouth. My cellie leaned back and nodded. In this world, certain details tell a whole story.

In some ways the underground criminal world is strange, yet it has rules that pass for honor. Certain facts speak louder than any story. Men can read your history from a few details and know what kind of fool or fighter you are. If you have done real years in certain yards and you are still breathing to tell it, people get the picture fast.

The news had already painted mine. Eleven at Parchman. A year out. Wanted on three banks. That bought me a measured respect at the door and the chance to earn the rest. I was not new to the game.

Every inmate, no matter the state, knows the hard places by name. Angola in Louisiana. Huntsville in Texas. San Quentin in California. Rikers and Attica in New York. Joliet in Illinois. Say a yard and a man will nod or wince. The map is written on our faces.

After me and my cellie talked, we stepped into the dayroom. TV humming. Chess and cards in motion. I needed to learn who was who. Prisons always have a pecking order, and somewhere in that stack is the alpha. You can spot him. He is the one who changes the channel without asking. The one with the newest state clothes. The one whose jokes get laughs, funny or not, because fear is an easy audience. He might keep his shirt off so the muscle talks before he does. He will watch without looking, measuring whether you are a threat to his crown or a problem for his income.

I have been in a lot of county jails and pens. I will say this with no fluff. I had never seen anything like Orleans Parish Prison. If you skipped the chow hall, they rolled a couple of pans into the block and left them. No line. No trays. Get yours how you can. That can go one of two ways. If order is not set, the weak do not eat. If the block has a fair hand on the ladle, people eat and keep moving. We were lucky. An old timer out of Angola ran the count. Everybody respected him, even the hitters. They called him Chicken Wing.

I respect Chicken Wing to this day. He kept it fair. In the mornings he counted the boiled eggs and passed them out even. At night he did the same with the two bologna sandwiches. It sounds small until you are hungry. Then it sounds like peace.

I stayed in O.P.P. nine days, then the papers came and the chains followed. Extradition back to Mississippi to stand trial for three banks. I was glad to leave Orleans Parish, not because where I was going held mercy, but because leaving meant the next step toward whatever judgment I had earned— and whatever grace God still had for me.

CHAPTER 16

IF YOU PLAY YOU HAVE TO PAY

Those old theater masks say it plain. One laughs. One cries. Laugh now and cry later. I had bet my soul against that fiddle God and lost. Time to pay the piper.

Federal marshals came from Jackson to haul me back. Bright, windy morning. I sat in the back, wrists cuffed, waist chained, ankles bit by irons, looking out the window at the same road I had taken to New Orleans. This time there would be no beach, no music, no party. Just miles and a long look at myself.

Three hours is a lot of thinking. I replayed every bad choice like a tape I could not stop. I pictured the time waiting on me somewhere behind a fence I did not get to choose. How many years. How far down. I counted who might stand by me once the water started pouring into the boat. Maybe two souls. Maybe none. No blame either way. The captain goes down with the ship, not the passengers.

Bond was a joke. Even if they offered it, I had fifteen dollars to my name and was not sure I owned that. I had burned through more than twenty thousand in a month and had nothing to show but a headache and a record.

Booking in Mississippi felt like a repeat with the volume turned up. Prints, photo, the insults to dignity that come with the strip and the squat. Spread your butt cheeks. Cough. Lift your nuts. Open your mouth. Stick your tongue out. A shower that smelled like chemicals. A scratchy uniform and a short phone call. I called my mother. Told her I was back, that I was breathing. God bless her, she asked when visiting day was. I asked the CO, told her the time. She told me she loved me and to pray.

I wished I could. God felt past far, beyond heaven, beyond hope. After everything I had done and everything I had been told about Him, I figured He was disappointed too. Who was I to ask for mercy. I said yes ma'am and hung up. They handed me a receipt for the one dollar and fifteen cents in my pocket. After torching twenty grand, I guess they decided to let me keep that.

The tier door clicked behind me and I saw a few faces I knew from Parchman. We shook hands. Someone pushed a pack of cigarettes into my palm. They said they had seen me on the news and hoped I would get away. That is the kind of love you get inside. It sounds crooked and comes from a true place.

I did not have to guess who was who or where the pecking order sat. We knew each other's past. We all knew the one rule. There are no rules. I wasted no time on making a shank, because I knew without a doubt that they all had one I settled in, kept my back straight, and slept like a log the first few nights. No beef. My mother and a brother came for a fifteen-minute glass visit. They left a little money on my books so I could hit commissary. My heart swelled with joy hearing them say they would be back. Small mercies stack up.

Time found a rhythm. Sleep in the day. Stay up at night. Chess. Pushups. Dips on the bunk. Sit-ups. A garbage bag full of water turned into a weight. I was out of shape and trying to tune the machine back up because in jail and prison it is not if, but when. Fights, stabbings, murders.

A man who is ready does not have to get ready." The voice from the old man stayed in my mind.

You learn a thousand small habits meant to keep you alive. You do not linger where you are exposed. You keep your balance, your eyes, your awareness. You stack the odds in quiet ways because one bad minute can define a year.

There are codes and war readiness. Like for instance, there are no 15–30 minute showers in prison because the longer you are in there, you are exposed and wet. You want to get in, lather up and rise off. Get out. I've even had to shower with my shower shoes on. I've witnessed many men get shanked by letting their guard down in the shower.

You don't wash your hair in the shower because you have to close your eyes. But if you do feel comfortable washing your hair, then rinse with your back to the wall. Lean your head back and wash your hair to keep shampoo and water out of your eyes.

When you go use the toilet to take a shit, you take your pants all the way off and your underwear and your boots or shoes back on. Then span your legs open as you sit to take your shit. This keeps you from tripping over your underwear or pants if you are attacked, because an inmate can simply step on your underwear and pants then butcher you. So many things in prison can be the difference of life or death, and to me, one more day in the land of the living is far better than a dirt nap any day.

Days became weeks. Weeks, months. A court-appointed lawyer showed up and said he wanted a psychological evaluation. I did not love the idea of talking to anybody about everything, but if writing or talking might help, I would try.

Let me digress to say this plain. In a lot of Black families there is a stigma around mental health. Folks say if you need a psychiatrist you are headed to the crazy house. Some of that is pride. Some of it is the weight we carry from generations. You survive by putting your head down and working. Doctors are for bones and blood, not the mind. Mothers do not get to take days off from holding a house together. So the lemons keep coming and the lemonade gets made. Salute to Black women who keep families standing when the wind howls.

That does not mean other folks do not carry their own storms. I am speaking from where I stand.

Sitting across from Dr. Womack, who kept asking me to be honest, I answered what I could. Some questions I refused because picking at those scars made the room tilt. I did not lie. I did not have it in me to pretend.

Another inmate and I got into it after he kept pushing buttons. I snapped. He ended up with a broken arm, a fractured skull and a number of stitches from the beating I gave him with a mop ringer. He went to the hospital, and I went to the hole.

They flew me to the Federal Medical Center in Fort Worth. Con Air, shackles and all. I told more of my life than I ever planned to tell. I came back to Mississippi, and a few weeks later they put me on the plane again because Dr. Womack believed I was carrying post-traumatic stress. This was before the country said the letters out loud every night on TV. Back then it lived mostly in quiet rooms and tight throats.

This time he wrote it down in black and white. PTSD.

I went to trial on a "temporary insanity" defense.

"Guilty."

The masks were right. Laugh now, cry later. I had played. It was time to pay.

CHAPTER 17

IF YOU PLAY YOU HAVE TO PAY

You cannot see me, but I am always present. Run as fast as you can, and you will never escape me. Fight me with all your strength, and you will never defeat me. I lie when I wish, but I can never be brought to trial. Who am I. I am the weight of tomorrow and the echo of yesterday. I am consequence.

My past had come to collect. I had laughed. Now it was my time to cry. Father Time stepped out of the wings and folded his arms. I had bet against the tune and lost. The piper waited.

"All rise. Honorable Judge Tom S. Lee."

The judge came out of chambers, sat, shuffled the papers, and looked over them in a quiet that made the room hold its breath.

"In case number 3:00-cr-__, United States versus David Spicer, the Court imposes sentence as follows.

Count one, life.

Count two, life.

Count three, one hundred twenty months.

Count four, life.

Count five, life.

Count six, one hundred twenty months.

Count seven, life.

Count eight, life.

Count nine, one hundred twenty months. Followed by three years of supervised release."

The gallery was full because I was not the only soul waiting on numbers. The words landed like bricks. I did the math in my head and it kept adding up to forever. I cleared my throat.

"Your Honor," I said, "you just gave me six life sentences and thirty years. And we are worried about three years of supervised release when I get out."

He peered over his glasses. The corners of his mouth moved. "Mr. Spicer, I see your point," he said. "I am bound by the law and the guidelines."

The gavel tapped. "Court is adjourned."

They led us back to the holdover. When a judge drops time like that, people start acting like they are at your funeral. Inmates go quiet. Family stares through you. In my case the feeling fit. On paper I had been buried alive with no parole.

Hopeless tried to climb my back. I would not give it the reins. The audience was still watching. Predators still hunt after the verdict. Buzzards circle whether the body is warm or cold. I put on my "just another day at the office" face and kept breathing even while my soul cried behind it. My knees wanted to argue with gravity. My heart beat fast enough to kill me and bring me back in the same minute.

I had known before trial that my odds were dust. A plea for life had been on the table. I could not make myself sign my own grave marker. Some men wear the tattoo 13½. Twelve jurors, one judge, and a half a chance. I had stood before twelve, faced one, and felt my chance break in half.

The marshals loaded us in the van. I was chained first and strapped far from the door. I guess they imagined me leaping from a moving vehicle and sprinting through traffic. If it was not for bad luck, I would have none. Still, I told myself to fold this hand and wait on the next deal. As long as I had breath, I had a shot. Somewhere in a future no one could see, maybe there was a royal flush with my name on it.

Word travels faster than wind behind bars. By the time the steel door clicked me back onto the block, my sentence had beaten me there. Men looked busy. Reading. TV. Phones. Really they were watching to see if I would explode, smash a screen, swing on someone, or crawl to my rack and pull a sheet over my face.

I did none of that. I heard the judge. My body had not caught up. I made a cup of coffee and took a slow drink. An old pen pal from Parchman looked me dead in the eye.

"Well, man," he said, "he did me like that. Imagine what he will do to you. Your jacket is from here to China."

Laughter ran across the tier like a small mercy. The room could breathe again. I wrote letters that night. I hit the floor and worked until my arms trembled. From that day forward the countdown started in my bones. Forty-five days, give or take, until they shipped me to a pen with higher fences and louder ghosts. I told myself what the old heads always said. A man who is ready does not have to get ready.

I was not done. Not with hope. Not with God. Not with the man I still believed I could become, even if the state had called me finished.

CHAPTER 18

UNITED STATES FEDERAL PENITENTIARY, ATLANTA

Atlanta Federal Penitentiary is one of the oldest federal prisons still standing. You see its brick bones on the History Channel, then you see it in person, and it feels like the years barely moved the needle on the outside. The roofs wear scars. The stone keeps its frown.

The place sits right in a neighborhood. Out front: Mrs. Winner's fried chicken, a fire station, a check-cashing joint with a liquor store beside it, row houses, a bus stop where regular life still keeps a schedule. No surprise it is a Black neighborhood. From the sidewalk you can measure the mood inside: heavy iron wheels on the doors, a concrete wall sixty feet up, built to keep society's problems contained and out of sight.

The bus curls to a side bay, a hangar door drops like a storage gate, and the ritual starts. Guards line the lane for intake and receiving. The first lesson is plain. They are in charge. Not you. Most of them look six-four and above, the kind of height that makes orders sound heavier.

The pace is slow, slower than the military but just as certain. Stand up. Wait. Your name is called. Shuffle forward. At the desk is a lieutenant with a file already open. Your photo, your charges, the time you carry, notes about affiliations, flags for past assaults. The gate pops. Names get read. You step up.

"Name."

"Number."

"Date of birth."

I heard "Spicer," and walked forward. "David Spicer, 27226-034. Nine twenty seventy." I was thirty-one. It was 2002. The bus spit us out two by two. Two guards patted me down, checked my ears, mouth, fingertips. They want to be sure nothing extra rode in.

There is always small talk during intake. It is not friendly. It is diagnostic.

"Where you from."

"Mississippi."

"You done time before."

"Yes, sir. Eleven years at Parchman."

"I heard about Parchman. They still picking cotton up there."

"Yes, sir."

"How long you down for, Spicer."

"Life."

"Damn, big man. Who you kill."

They already knew the answer. Files get read like textbooks. The questions are a temperature check, a way to see how you carry yourself and whether they will have to repeat the rules you already know by heart.

When you are done, they turn you to face the wall. Two reasons. First, less chance you do something foolish when backs turn. Second, it tests compliance. There is always a man who must do the opposite, the one who will not face the wall, the man who thinks rules are for other people. He will meet a lesson one way or another. You learn early to step away from that kind of gravity.

The guards may not beat his ass, but he may get a cellmate at the time who loves to fight or may engage in man-on-man loving. He is too blind and too dumb to notice the guards keep looking his way. This is a guy you start to quickly disassociate yourself from because he has a very hard lesson to learn, and you don't want him thinking that you are his buddy. The lesson he has to learn may cost him his life. He thinks he knows everything, so you can't tell him anything. You can't help him. Don't even try.

They lead us single file into the concrete maze. Designated holding. Strip. Shower. Medical. Psych. Forms. The questions come like a checklist.

"Any medical problems?"

"Any prescriptions?"

"Are you okay right now?"

"Any mental-health history? Do you feel like hurting yourself or anyone else?"

Then the paperwork stack: you understand mail will be opened and may be read. You understand phone calls are monitored and recorded. You received the A and O handbook. You spoke to medical. You feel stable.

Next, the classification script: Have you ever testified against anyone. Do you fear someone in general population. Tattoos. Where. Any affiliations. Jewelry. Do you want to send your street clothes home or surrender them. Sign here. And here. All of this covers the institution and, at least on paper, tries to steer you toward the safest placement they can justify. Where you land—protective custody or population—rides on those answers and on what their file already says.

A CO hands out brown-bag lunches. The standard kit: a sandwich with mystery meat or peanut butter, chips or crackers, a small juice, a piece of fruit. "Hot meal next chow," someone says like it is a promise.

After we eat, they move us to intake segregation for a seventy-two-hour observation. The pause serves four purposes. One, your new cellie will tell you what you need to know about the yard—who is who, how things run, what not to do. Two, if you rolled in with anything in your system, the clock gives your body time to clear it. Three, your nerves can catch up to the reality of the walls. Four, staff gets a read on whether you can function in population without setting the unit on fire.

Seventy-two hours ticked past, and I met the captain. He looked over my jacket and nodded.

"I see you know how to do time already," he said. "Go do it."

Thirty minutes later I was walking into general population to start a life sentence. The door closes behind me with the crash of my futuret.

CHAPTER 19

A WORLD WITHIN A WORLD

I read once that writing was born from our inability to sit still. Prison cures that the hard way. You sit because steel says so.

Six a.m. The doors pop and men burst out like a starter's bell just rang. It is "breakfast," but the tier is its own street market. Coffee hisses in jailhouse kettles. Dice whisper in corners. Some men are cooking, some are nodding, some are scanning the crowd with hunter eyes because sleep sharpened their teeth. Somewhere, two men lean close and call it love. Somewhere else a whisper becomes a plot.

I kept low. For the moment I had a single cell and the quiet that comes with it. Word travels fast in a cage. "Mississippi," they said, and my home state found me. In prison there is an unspoken rule: when a man from your soil hits the yard, you put a little wind in his sail: Soap, toothpaste, Shower shoes, a scoop of coffee, or a few smokes back when tobacco was still a thing. You pay it forward to the next one through the gate. We call it a blessing.

If your homeboys are winning the yard, you can tell by the care packages. We called it 200S and wham-whams. States try to outdo other states the way teams try to outscore teams. You represent where you are from.

Federal time is different from state time. States pen you by counties and lines. Feds run on "cars." A car is who you ride with. I am Mississippi, which makes me Southern by default. Louisiana, Texas, Florida, Alabama, Mississippi, Tennessee. We move as one if it goes left. Other cars move as one too. Some are built around race and symbols. Some around cities. Some around money. Most days nothing breaks. Some days everything does, but the next day, the chow line is back to normal like a storm never blew through.

You still have to watch who you sit with, who you vouch for, who eats at your table. There are men you cannot stand next to; no exceptions. No rapist or child molesters are allowed—period. If you sponsor the wrong man, you inherit his enemies and his shame.

I spent my first stretch learning names and angles, who runs which car, who fronts and who really stands up, who moves contraband. Who loans and collects, keeps a little store under the bunk, who is hungry and who hunts hungry men. I quickly bought four shanks. Why four?

Because even though I was not going to carry all four at one time, you always need to have shanks in different parts of the prison. I took one shank and stuck it in the ground. Not too deep, but just enough to be out of sight. That's called "burying your bone."

When the doors open in the morning, a smart man learns the map before the map learns him. I did my laps. I felt the eyes. I found the corners that fit my back

Protection is a fact of life in a place like this. I made sure I had what I needed and made sure it was where I could reach it without getting myself into more trouble. In prison, the thing that keeps you safe is not bravado, it is preparation.

It did not take long before I needed it—twice.

CHAPTER 20

PUTTING IN WORK

In prison, "putting in work" means handling business through violence. Everyone knows it. No one has to say how.

Cash is contraband in the feds, so the yard runs on substitutes. Stamps, commissary, reputation. Tobacco used to be king until they killed it. That only pushed the black-market price higher on anything still moving. A single pack could float near a hundred dollars in street money, no credit, no tabs. People wired funds through the free world. A go-between checked the receipt, and goods changed hands.

A cellmate may have a thousand books of stamps. But by policy he is only supposed to have three books. He got them from hustling. He may be the big dope man on the yard. He may be the loan shark or the bookie. Now add that

1,000 book stamps x $8.00 from the commissary — that's $8,000. Now 1,000 books at 25 books for $100 = $4,000 of his pocket. Not a bad day's work for no work.

Folks say there is no honor among thieves. That is not true in here. Honor and trust are the grease that keeps this broke machine turning. If you burn a man on a deal, you might not get killed, but you will lose business, protection, and sleep. In a cage, those are three ways to starve.

There was An O.G. who went by several nicknames: "Crash Dummy," "Dead Man Walking," and "Big Mouth Bass" — just to name a few. He ran a common yard scam. He would find someone and offer them a sweet bet. He put up $200 to another man's $100. But the other inmate would have to give him the point spread out of Las Vegas that's in the news paper.

They bet on "fi'e," meaning they had no intention of paying if the line went bad. If the bet hit, they collected from ten different men at once. If it missed, they swore the money never landed. Pull that on a timid guy and he pays twice to dodge trouble.

Crash Dummy ran this on my homeboy. But he fucked up because my homeboy was not a weak inmate. He's was small in size and some inmates mistake short size as a sign of weakness.

My homeboy refused to pay. Once my homeboy refused to pay him a second time, he walked down on the yard, which means "Dead man walking." Crash Dummy had no choice but to put a hit out on my homeboy to send the message. If he let it slide, the other inmates will see him as weak.

Crash Dummy and another one of his grimy buddies caught my homeboy at work in the bathroom and stabbed him bad. When asked who attacked him, my homeboy refused to snitch, so Crash Dummy and his buddy got away. But in prison the administration always knows what's happening, but they understand the laws of the concrete jungle. Inmates who don't tell have their own form of justice planned.

Normally I stay out of men's pockets. If you play and do not pay, you accept the tax. But he had paid. I was going to handle this one myself.

I decided to wait a few weeks. I kept my peace and let time cool the glare. Some messages carry farther when they arrive late. I needed him to think he had gotten away so he would drop his guard and I could rock him to sleep.

Just like I expected, he never saw me coming. In federal prison each unit has three main washers and dryers and a main laundry. Each unit has an industrial size laundry cart. If you needed your laundry done, you could just throw it in the cart at breakfast and the unit orderly would push the laundry cart down to the laundry.

Crash Dummy worked in the laundry. I paid the orderly to let me get in the laundry basket, cover me up with the dirty laundry, and push me into the laundry room. I took my shanks out of my cell because I knew I wasn't coming back to that cell. I did not want the next inmate to occupy that cell to get charged for it if it was found. It was around 10:00 a.m.

I could hear him joking with inmates as he pass, relaxed and unguarded, just like I wanted him. The orderly pushed me up the ramp.

"okay, I'll see y'all at 3 o'clock." I heard the orderly say.

He left and I waited maybe 10–15 minutes. Then someone pushed the cart I was hiding in into the laundry. I waited until I did not hear another voice, and got out. I had my shanks wrapped around my hands to keep from dropping them. Shanks get slippery when blood is on them.

I made my way to the front. I was going to try to make sure he lived up to his nickname "Dead Man Walking."

He was talking with his back to me. He bent over to step around the laundry machines. Like a black opps soldier, I came up silently behind and stabbed him with both of my shanks. Once his mind registered what was happening, he began screaming and trying to run. I gave chase stabbing him all along the way.

Everyone got out of the way. The laundry supervisor must have hit his body alarm because the alarms went off and I could hear feet pounding the pavement coming my way. So I ran to the bathroom because I was covered in blood. I needed to wash off my shanks.

They came in while I was trying to flush the shanks that would not flush. The guards told me to get on the floor. I did and they cuffed me, took me to the hole. I could hear the blaring siren of the ambulance coming to get O.G. Mouth Bass, a.k.a. "Crash Dummie" as I walk to the hole. World Memorial was about to get one more name on a plaque.

I had sent the message that needed sending. "#21262034 was **not** taking any wooden nickels."

CHAPTER 21

DECLARING WAR

If you walk into the hole, the SHU, you step into a madhouse. Men talk over each other, cussing, singing, preaching. The mentally ill bang metal like it is a drum line. Doors rattle. Voices ricochet.

When the entrance door pops and a CO escorts someone in from the compound, the noise pauses the way a storm pauses. Everyone cranes to see who is coming down the tier, to guess what just happened on the yard, to figure out if they know you or know someone who knows you. Then the shouting starts again.

"Open cells," men call. "Try fourteen. Try six."

A decent cellie can mean the difference between life and death.

Most COs try to place you where two men can coexist, mostly because they do not want to break up fights all shift. They stripped me out of the bloody clothes, and SIS bagged them for evidence. They already knew what this was–Payback. I asked where my homeboy was. Luck for me, he had a single.

They walked me to his door, killed the lights, and told him he was getting a celly.

"Get yo ass up and make me some coffee," I called.

He laughed, and they cuffed him so I could come in.

In the SHU, they cuff you before they open a door. Two reasons: So no one swings on staff. So no one gets jumped while their hands are useless. Once the cuffs come off, it is on you. Good luck, God bless, every man for himself.

My homeboy grinned when I stepped in. He knew why I was there. We hugged and dapped and I gave him the play-by-play of what went down. He forgot all about his bandages for a second and bounced like a cheer captain. I had carried the message he could not send, and in that small square of concrete and steel, it felt like justice finally found our door.

He went into his mattress and got me two shanks. He was waiting until he fully heeled because Crush Dummy had some crazy brothers over in the hole and one of them was on the same rec schedule as he was. He was going to hit him.

So without any doubt, I was on. See in prison, once you have beef with a ward or group of guys there is never any peace between you and them.

War was declared.

You try to hit them before they hit you. It does not matter that the rest of his gang was not involved with the situation. In prison, you're guilty by association. That's just the law of the streets. So ole boy had to get his share of the punishment.

They thought having me and my homeboy chilled a couple of months would bring the peace. They were wrong. As soon as my homeboy healed, we went out to rec and shanked Crash Dummie's friend. That was my second stabbing in a few months so I knew the administration was going to take a heavy hand with me this time.

I was right. They re-pulled me from everyone else's cell above rec alone. I was headed to Marion, IL.

CHAPTER 22

Welcome to Hell

After a couple of years in the hole they stamped me "maximum." I sat on hold waiting out transfers through places like ADX Florence in Colorado, the joint they love to mention whenever they talk terrorists on the news. Around 2006 they changed Marion to a medium. Before that, Marion wore the nickname "the new Alcatraz." Names like John Gotti and Jeff Fort had passed through those doors. The reputation arrived before the bus.

From the road Marion looks quiet. Trees. Low buildings. A hush that pretends to be peaceful. Up close it is something else. Two officers for every inmate. Batons that gleam. Black uniforms posted with long guns. A CO pointed to the towers and said, "Right now you got snipers on you through glass. Try something stupid." Ankles in irons, wrists in cuffs locked inside a black box, belly chain tight. You learn how small a man can feel while still filling out his own shadow.

They staged us in a holding run, maybe ten of us off that trip. Then they called names and moved us into a second room swimming with officers. They put each man on a wooden block in the center. They circled. Orders came fast. "Take off your clothes." Naked, you keep your eyes fixed on a seam in the wall and you answer clean.

"Answer the captain, boy."

"Yes, sir, Captain."

"You think you tough."

"No, sir."

"You like to stab people, Spicer."

"No, sir."

"You better not touch one of my officers. You understand."

"Yes, sir."

In that room there was not a Black officer in sight. Tobacco in cheeks. Dipping cups. The message was simple. Your life is one breath away if we decide it is. Fifteen minutes feels like an hour when your dignity is on the floor. They tossed me a red jumpsuit, no underwear, no T-shirt, one pair of shower shoes that might as well have been size "who cares," and walked me into the machine.

Mug shot. Paperwork. The file already knew me. Nicknames. Past time. Every address I ever slept at. They did not need my fingerprints to prove a point. The point was that I was marked. Medical was a box on a form, not a person. If you got sick, they believed an old-fashioned beating could cure it. They asked the snitch question. They always do.

"Are you willing to be our eyes and ears."

"No, sir."

"Why did you stab those people." I told them my why. They nodded like it was weather and sent me to segregation for thirty days of observation.

The cell at Marion is a closet that grew a toilet. Concrete slab for a bed. A mattress thin enough to fold inside a book. A light that hummed. A steel bowl with no shelf. You can stand with your back to one wall and touch the other with your fingertips. Heat sits heavy. There is no air conditioning. The windows are cut in a way that lets mosquitoes clock in for the night shift. Showers are supposed to be three times a week. You get four minutes, timed. Most men skip and take a bird bath. You lean over the toilet, fill a little bucket, soap up, and rinse the anger off your skin before lockdown.

Mail comes like a rumor. They might hold it two months. They might mix your outgoing letters so the wrong person reads the right pain. They might "lose" it. You complain to the sky. The sky does not write back. Who believes a tier full of inmates over a badge and a logbook.

Marion is designed to humiliate you, starve you of the outside, and break you into pieces small enough to stack. I learned to count the pieces and keep them in my pocket like stones. I learned to pray without moving my lips. I learned to listen for my own heartbeat in a place that swears it can take it from you.

The days in Marion blurred into a calendar of small cruelties. You learn to measure time by sound the clank of a tray, the footstep of a guard, the rustle of someone folding a letter. Any trouble that came my way, I was going to quickly and swiftly meet it by sending the other person to the graveyard.

I was coming from the commissary one day, and three gang members approached me and asked me to give them some commissary. I told them, no. One raised his shirt, showing me his shank, and told me they would come see me later and take it. That was his first mistake.

See, I had a couple of simple rules that I always lived by in prison. Do not threaten me and do not put your hands on me. If you do one of those two, I do not care if the President of the United States is there, I'm going to try to take your life.

I went to my housing unit, entered my cell, put my commissary in my locker, locked it and cooked a concoction of baby oil, sugar, comic, and heated it up in the microwave. I was watching him and the the other gang members. They are paying me no attention. I had already fought the fight in my mind.

I walked through the assault. I would scald him by throwing the burning concoction in his face. I would take the shank he flashed and stab him to death with it. And that's exactly what I did.

It's hard to explain. I was hitting him in every place that I could: his neck, his chest. Somehow I had a grip on this shank, but it was like someone took my hand, opened it and threw the knife across the room. But the other gang members were standing, frozen watching the fight.

I quickly got up to get the shank because I did not want any of the other gang members to get it and kill me. When I got up off of him, he ran out of the unit and the police quickly locked the door.

They put me back in the hole for two years. Solid white walls. One light that never quit. No cellmate. No music. Just the sound of a clock and my own breath. For eighteen months I lived in that smallness until they told us Marion was changing into a terrorist unit. They packed us and moved us again, next stop ADX Florence, Colorado.

CHAPTER 23

ADX

The ADX Supermax is designed to house what was considered the worst of the worst federal prisoners. They house terrorists, gang leaders, gang members, people from different state prisons that their state couldn't control and just high profile people. I was serving time with Rudolph, the Atlanta City, bomber; Jeff Ford; Larry Hoover andTerry Nichols.

The cell was another form of torturee. 4 x 4. You walk four steps to your sink, four steps to the bars, four steps back to the bed. The cells are concrete shells with a TV in the wall and a small slot for chow. They do everything they can to keep you inside the skin of your box. Medical comes to you. Commissary comes to you. The man you were meets the man you are and neither one wants to talk.

Year after year, I walked those four steps to my bars, to the shower, to the bars, to the bed. The rhythm became a slow heartbeat that kept time with my own. In that endless repetition, I saw men give up. I saw the bright quickness of life fade from their eyes until they were only bodies moving through routine.

One morning started like any other. The halls of ADX were quiet except for the metallic click of food slots and the low hum of fluorescent light. I was halfway through my pushups when I heard it: shouting down the range. A C.O. ran past my door. Another followed. Doors slammed. Radios crackled.

The noise echoed through the concrete, a ripple in the silence that usually never changed. A crackling voice said through the walkie talkie, "Is he gone?" The officer returned, "Yes sir."

I froze. For months I had talked to the prisoner next to me through the vents about life, freedom, and the little things that kept us sane: music we missed, food we dreamed about, what we'd do if we ever saw sunlight without bars in the way.

They rolled a stretcher past, a white sheet pulled tight. The guards' faces were carved out of stone.

I stood at my door and whispered his name into the silence. It was Christmas Day. Somewhere outside these walls people were unwrapping gifts, eating, laughing. In here, death had come wrapped in a sheet.

That night, the air felt heavier. The unit smelled like bleach. I sat on the edge of my bunk and stared at the ceiling, trying to pray but no words came out. I only remember the sound of the ventilation system carrying my heartbeat back to me like a slow, broken echo.

Now, I know some people who are reading this book or listening will say, well, it's jail, it's prison. You are supposed to lose your rights. To some extentent, I agree. But we need to change that mentality and realize that even though we made mistakes, committed crimes, we are still humans.

Long stories short, 90% of most inmates in jails and prisons are going to be released. But it's because of the mistreatment, the beatings, the bad food, that some inmates develop suicidal or serial killer mentalities.

Suicide moves like a shadow: quiet, patient, waiting. It doesn't care who you are, how strong you think you are, or how many battles you've already fought. Some nights, I could hear it whispering through the vents.

Then came the letter. The C.O. slid it through the slot without a word. I opened it expecting routine words from home. Instead, it was five words that broke me in half:

"Your mother passed last night."

The paper trembled in my hands. The walls pressed in until it felt like the whole cell was closing its fist around me. I sat on the edge of my bunk and read the lines again, hoping the words would rearrange themselves, hoping there was some mistake.

But the truth was as still as the concrete. She was gone. For hours, I couldn't move. My chest hurt, but no tears came. Just silence. I felt a hole open inside me so wide it swallowed every word I had ever prayed.

That night, I lay staring at the ceiling, counting cracks that weren't there, thinking of the woman who raised me to believe in God. But I didn't believe anymore. I couldn't. Not in that place. The thought came slow, calm, and cold: *Maybe the only way out is to stop breathing.*

I didn't say it out loud. I just felt it, and for the first time, I understood how a man could decide that the fight wasn't worth it anymore.

CHAPTER 24

Light in the Darkness

A psychiatrist named Dr. Garber kept coming by my cell. She did not move like the others. She brought books. She asked me to write. I refused at first. I remember the first essay I wrote for her. It was two pages about an orange tree I used to see from my grandmother's porch. When she read it she smiled like she had found a small country inside me.

Slowly, she earned my trust. She kept her promises. If she said she would be back at noon, she was back at noon. She did not sugarcoat things. She said, "Tell the truth and the truth will tell you where to stand."

One morning I was on a hunger strike. She came and talked me off it by solving a problem that technically was not hers to fix. After that she had currency with me. We talked for hours. When I walked back to my cell after one of those talks I felt like something had been lifted.

A night came when I broke down in my bunk. Guards pushed a breakfast slot and I screamed, "Call Dr. Garber." The guards broke from their usual calloused disregard and rushed to get her on the phone.

She ran into my unit and sat on the metal chair and talked to me until the air came back into my chest. She talked me out of killing myself.

Those small conversations began to stitch something back together within me. I started to pray because that is what my mother taught me to do. I read Genesis and stopped on Joseph. A man who sat in prison and still rose became a map for me.

In my spiritual darkness, a small glimmer of light forced its way through. It was a strange, unusual belief that I could be free. It was strange, but I felt confident that even though I had been sentenced to 6 life sentences, somehow I would be freed.

Over the next seven years, I changed my life and started living for God. Interesting thought, that a man who spends 23 hours a day in a 4 x 4 cell could claim to be "living" for God, but salvation is within your spirit, not your day to day activities. My heart had completely changed.

I started watching Bishop T. D. Jakes' and other pastors on Sundays. I even started paying tithes to Jakes' church. The words of another man who had been through storms began to sit in my chest like bread. Faith was not a light switch. It came slow and stubborn.

That night, the cell felt different. It was too still, too heavy. I lay on my bunk staring at the cracked ceiling, tracing the faint shadow of the bars as the moonlight slid across them. Somewhere between the hum of the vent and the shuffle of guards down the corridor, I drifted into a dream.

In it, I was walking down a narrow path, dirt under my feet, fog curling around my legs like smoke. I didn't know where I was headed, but something, someone, was calling my name. Then a voice broke through the mist, clear and certain.

"Write a motion to dismiss your charges."

I turned, searching for where it came from. The fog parted, and I saw a courtroom rise up around me. The marble floors gleamed, and the wood was polished to a holy shine. I stood in chains before a judge who looked down at me not with anger, but with understanding.

"This man," the judge said, his gavel raised, "should be freed immediately."

The sound of the gavel cracked like thunder. I woke up sweating, my heart slamming against my ribs. The cell was still dark, but I could feel the echo of that dream running through me.

"A motion to dismiss?" I muttered to myself, shaking my head. "That's crazy."

I sat on the edge of the bunk, rubbing my hands together. How could I write something like that? I was guilty. I didn't deserve clemency. Who was I to ask for freedom?

The idea seemed foolish; too wild to believe. I tried to brush it off, tried to tell myself it was just a dream. But even as I lay back down, the judge's voice lingered, heavy and alive, like it had come from somewhere beyond sleep.

Days later, I stood at the small metal sink, brushing my teeth in slow circles, watching the foam swirl down the drain. The pipes groaned, the air smelled faintly of bleach, and somewhere down the tier a radio played low gospel music.

Then I heard it again.

"You still have not filed that motion."

The voice was calm, steady, and close enough that I turned around expecting someone to be standing behind me. No one was there. Just the hum of fluorescent lights and the distant echo of footsteps.

I spat into the sink and stared at my reflection. "I'm losing my mind," I whispered.

After breakfast, I sat on the edge of my bunk, sipping bitter coffee from a chipped cup. The smell of it mixed with the scent of disinfectant. I opened my tattered copy of *Jesus Is Calling* and read a few lines, words about obedience and faith that felt aimed right at me. My hands trembled a little as I closed the book.

"Alright, God," I said quietly. "If this is You, give me the words."

I had never been to law school. I didn't know the first thing about legal procedure. But something in me pushed past the fear. I pulled out a pen and a few sheets of lined paper, sat under the dim light, and began to write.

The words came slowly at first, then all at once, like water breaking through a dam. I filled three pages by hand, folded them neatly, and slipped them into an envelope.

When the mail cart came by that afternoon, I handed it over. My heart pounded as the officer wheeled it away, unaware that somewhere inside that stack of letters was a motion I had written by faith alone.

CHAPTER 25

Free: Mind, Body, and Soul

Thirty days passed in the slow rhythm that only prison can teach. Each day carried the same metallic clatter of doors, the same hollow footsteps in the corridor, the same bitter taste of coffee poured from the same dented pot. I had learned how to make peace with sameness. I didn't expect surprises here.

Then one morning a counselor appeared at my cell with a clipboard pressed against his chest. His look told me this was not another routine check-in. "Spicer," he said, jerking his chin toward the hallway, "walk with me."

We moved down the corridor side by side, our footsteps echoing off concrete walls. The air was stale and heavy, filled with the faint hum of fluorescent lights. In his office the blinds hung crooked, a slow-moving fan pushed warm air in small circles, and stacks of old paperwork leaned against the corners. He gestured for me to sit.

"You got a call," he said, flipping a few pages on his clipboard. "Public defender out of Jackson, Mississippi. Name's Jacinta Hall. She asked to refile your motion."

The words didn't sound real at first. "She read what I wrote?"

"She did," he said. "She wants to talk to you herself."

He handed me the phone. I gripped the receiver tight, the cord coiling between my fingers like a live thing. For a moment I wondered if this was some kind of joke. Then the line clicked, and a woman's voice filled my ear—steady, confident, with the kind of calm you can feel even when you can't see the person speaking.

"Mr. Spicer? This is Jacinta Hall with the public defender's office in Jackson. Thank you for taking my call."

"Thank you for calling," I said slowly. "I'm still trying to believe this is real."

"I saw your motion," she said. "You filed it on your own?"

"Yes," I told her. "Three pages by hand. I didn't know the rules or how to word it right. I just... wrote what I believed."

"I'd like to refile it properly," she said. "Can you tell me in your own words what led you to write it?"

I hesitated, feeling heat rise to my face. Then I told her. I told her about the dream, about hearing a voice that told me to write a motion to dismiss my charges. I told her how foolish it sounded and how I wrote it anyway because faith sometimes sounds foolish. When I finished, the line went quiet. I thought she had hung up.

Then she said softly, "I don't think you're crazy. My father is a pastor. I believe you."

For a second I couldn't speak. My throat tightened, and the world around me blurred. It had been years since anyone said they believed me. The words sank into me like sunlight through cold water.

"Thank you," I whispered.

"We'll be in touch soon," she said. "You did the hard part already."

When the call ended, I sat staring at the desk. The sound of the fan and the ticking of the wall clock filled the space between us. I walked back to my cell in a haze. That night, lying on my bunk, I replayed her voice in my head until sleep finally took me.

But hope changes time. Before that call, the days were flat and painless in their emptiness. After it, every hour cut deeper. Waiting became its own kind of suffering. I started counting days again, which was something I had long stopped doing. I watched every mail call like a starving man waiting for bread. Even silence became heavier because now it had meaning. Before, silence meant nothing. Now it meant waiting.

Weeks crawled by. I went through my routine trying not to let the hope show on my face. I swept floors, lined up for meals, and read the same few pages of my worn Bible until the print blurred. At night I would whisper, "God, if that was really You, keep moving." Sometimes I almost believed I could feel something shifting, a current under the surface.

Then one afternoon, during mail call, the officer's voice carried down the tier like a stone skipping across water.

"Spicer!"

He slid a thick white envelope through the slot. The paper was heavy, the kind used by people who never had to wonder if their letters would make it to the other side. I turned it over. The return address made my breath hitch.

Simpson Thacher & Bartlett LLP. New York.

I stared at it for a long time before opening it, my fingers tracing the raised ink of the letterhead. The other men were watching me through their doors, whispering guesses about what it was. My cellmate said, "That looks official, man."

"Yeah," I said quietly. "Real official."

I tore the envelope open carefully and unfolded the letter inside. My eyes scanned the first line, then the second. The words hit me one by one, each heavier than the last. *We are writing to inform you that our firm will be representing you in partnership with the Mississippi Public Defender's Office. This representation will be provided pro bono.*

My mouth went dry. I read it twice, then a third time, making sure it said what I thought it said. Then I laughed out loud, unguarded, the kind of laugh that breaks through a man's ribs. My cellmate jumped at the sound.

"What happened?" he called out.

"They're taking my case," I said, grinning. "A world-class law firm in New York is taking my case for free."

He let out a long whistle. "Man, you must got God's private number."

"Maybe He called collect," I said, and we both laughed until my chest hurt. Then, when the noise faded, I sat back down on the bunk and read the letter again. There was something holy about the way the words sat on the page. It didn't promise victory, only motion—movement where there had been none.

That night, I tucked the letter inside my Bible and stared at the ceiling until the lights went out. For the first time in decades, I fell asleep smiling.

The motion was officially filed on November 10, 2021. I marked the date in the margin of my Bible and tried to let go of the need to know what would happen next. But it is impossible to have a spark of hope and not feel its absence when days stretch on without word. Time after that slowed to a crawl.

Winter came and went, the yard covered in frost that cracked beneath our shoes. Spring arrived with a pale sun that did little to warm the yard. Every knock on my door made my pulse jump. I tried to convince myself that peace meant trusting the process, but trust is harder than steel when you've lived your life behind it.

Nine months later, on August 10, 2022, I was in the cell doing sit-ups. The volume of the TV was low. The voice of whatever preacher was preaching at the time was ambient noise added to the the background rhythm of prisoners talking across cells and spoons clinking against metal cups. I wasn't thinking about much of anything when the officer walked up.

"Spicer," he said, flat and official. "We need a name and phone number for where you're being released to."

For a second, I thought I'd misheard. "Say again?"

Slightly agitated, the guard repeated slower this time. "Name and phone number. You're being released."

The room fell away. I could hear my pulse in my ears. I stood, gripping the edge of the metal table to steady myself. My voice trembled as I spoke my brother's name and number. The next few minutes stretched into something that didn't feel like time at all. I watched the clock until it felt like the second hand might tear from its pin.

Then, the clicking echo of footsteps came down the hall.

I whispered a prayer. "Lord please don't let him tell me it was a mistake. I don't think I can bear it."

"Pack up, Spicer. The judge ordered your immediate release. You have to be off the grounds by five o'clock."

"What?" I yelled with excitement.

"You want to stay?" The guard said with a slight grin. "We can make that happen."

"No sir! I screamed with delight. Keep it all, I can go right now!"

I packed like a man who'd been given back his lungs after years underwater. I gathered my letters, and tucked the

Bible with the letter still inside it on top. Men along the tier watched as I walked down the hall with my bag. Some nodded, some smiled, and a few whispered prayers. Everyone knew what that walk meant.

At the gate, a guard double-checked my papers. The final lock clicked open. The sound was small but heavy enough to shake the world.

When I stepped outside, sunlight hit me full in the face. The sky stretched wider than I remembered, blue and endless. I stopped and drew in a deep breath, air filling every corner of my chest. The taste of it was sharp and clean. For the first time in more than three decades, I felt alive.

A van idled nearby, ready to take me to processing. Beyond the fence a line of trees swayed gently, leaves rustling like applause. I stared at them and let the moment wash through me. I didn't cry, not because I wasn't moved, but because tears felt too small for what was happening.

When the officer at processing read the order aloud, his tone shifted halfway through, as if he suddenly realized what he was saying. The same judge who had once sentenced me to six life terms now wrote that he would never have done so had he known the full circumstances. The court had granted immediate release.

I signed the forms one by one, each signature like a heartbeat. When they handed me the small envelope with my belongings—an ID, a few letters, one photograph—I tucked it into my pocket and waited for the final nod.

At 4:57 p.m., I stepped through the outer gate. The air was warm and golden. The horizon looked like something alive. I stood there a long time, not wanting to move. The gravel under my shoes, the smell of sun on metal, the sound of wind through open space—all of it felt like proof.

I walked forward slowly, breathing deep.

For the first time in my life, I was truly free, mind, body, and soul.

DEDICATION

1 dedicate this book to. My Lord and Savior Jesus Christ, my mother who never gave up on me, Dr. Garner, ADX psychiatrist. And last but never least!! My beautiful queen and wife Verleria Spicer. I love you with a love that's heavenly

www.ingramcontent.com/pod-product-compliance
Lightning Source LLC
Chambersburg PA
CBHW032059020426
42335CB00011B/406